M000086757

PEACE, YA DIG

Created by Copyright Éditions
104, boulevard Arago
75014 Paris - France

Original concept: Olo Éditions
Editorial direction: Laura Stioui
Editors: Claudie Souchet and Sara Quémener,
assisted by Mathilde Boisserie
Translator: Roland Glasser
Art direction: Émilie Greenberg
Graphic design: Élise Godmuse
Layout: Thomas Hamel
Copyediting: Sabine Jean
Image editing: Thomas Hamel and Cédric Delsart
Production: Stéphanie Parlange and Cédric Delsart

English typesetting and cover design by Kayleigh Jankowski

First published in the United States of America in 2017
by Universe Publishing
A Division of Rizzoli International Publications, Inc.
300 Park Avenue South
New York, NY 10010
www.rizzoliusa.com

Originally published in French in 2016 by Éditions de La Martinière,
an imprint of EDLM
www.editionsdelamartiniere.fr

All rights reserved. No part of this book may be reproduced, stored in
a retrieval system, or transmitted, in any form or by any means, electronic,
mechanical, photocopying, recording, or otherwise, without prior consent
of the publishers.

2017 2018 2019 2020 / 10 9 8 7 6 5 4 3 2 1

ISBN: 978-0-7893-3279-0

Library of Congress Control Number: 2016954666

Printed in Malaysia

Note: All the T-shirts shown are based on a single model (in order to ensure
a uniform appearance) designed by us to be as realistic as possible.

1000
T-SHIRTS
THAT MAKE A STATEMENT

Raphaëlle Orsini

UNIVERSE

CONTENTS

158

TV & MOVIE CULTURE:
COTTON ON SCREEN

186

TRIBE:
IDENTITY T-SHIRTS

200

SPORTS: TEAM UNIFORMS

216

FASHION VICTIM:
ON THE RED CARPET

236

ARTY:
WEAR CREATIVITY

T-SHIRTS
FOR LIFE

Everyone has at least one T-shirt. Perhaps it has been sleeping peacefully at the back of the closet for many years, or maybe it was the latest impulse buy. Some people don't give their T-shirts a second thought, while others elevate them to cult status. One person will happily lend his or hers to a friend, while another will pass it on to his or her son or daughter, and some will guard theirs jealously like personal treasures. Whatever it is and whatever it represents, everybody has one. There is something quite intimate about the relationship we have with a T-shirt. It is something to be trusted. It is what we wear when we've run out of clean laundry, or when we want to simply be ourselves, or when we require reassurance and solace.

As it ages, we like to sniff its soft cotton fibers, smoothed by umpteen wash cycles. We appreciate the way its cut has taken the shape of our body, the particular manner in which the color has faded, the frayed collar betraying its age. We love to snuggle into it to sleep on a winter's night, or abuse it on a summer's day through repeated exposure to sunscreen and saltwater. The neutral odor of a still-new T-shirt is like a blank page, full of promise. We wear it proudly, like a trophy, full of desire to experience new adventures. A T-shirt says much about our relationship with the world and with fashion. It can suggest a quiet, introverted nature or a loud, outgoing one. It displays our musical, social, political, and stylistic tastes. In short,

the humble T-shirt very much expresses a part of our identity. And if everyone has at least one T-shirt, it's because the T-shirt is a monument, a kind of holy object that has experienced all eras and styles, without flinching.

The plain cotton T-shirt has become the most worn garment of all time, shaking up the fashion world. But, more than the fashion world, it is the whole of society that has been turned upside down. For the T-shirt can be a political banner, a professional uniform, a mark of a music fan's passion, a sign of identity, or a promotional poster. It is worth almost nothing in and of itself, and can be sold in mass quantities, yet certain T-shirts are museum pieces, luxury items reserved for a select few. The T-shirt is a social, cultural, generational, and experimental thing. It is the mirror of a moment, of an era, of our realties and our fantasies. The T-shirt has multiple facets, which is no doubt why it is eternal. We all have at least one T-shirt, and we all know how much it means to us.

T-SHIRT STATS

N° 1

China is the biggest producer of cotton (ahead of India and the United States). *

5¼ OUNCES

Approximate weight of an adult T-shirt.

10 SECONDS

The I Love NY T-shirt is the best-selling garment in the world, with one sold every ten seconds.

2 BILLION

Number of T-shirts sold globally each year. *

1913

Year that the white T-shirt, with short sleeves and a collar hugging the neck, became part of the United States Navy uniform.

$91,500

The price of the most expensive T-shirt in the world, made of black crocodile skin, from the brand Hermès.

$20 BILLION

Amount spent on T-shirts in the United States in 2014.

305 FT 9¼ IN

The largest T-shirt in the world is 305 feet 9¼ inches long by 205 feet 9½ inches wide. It was unveiled by Equilibrios Camisetas Promocionais (Brazil) in Navegantes, Santa Catarina, Brazil, on October 11, 2014.

14 OUNCES

Amount of cotton fiber needed to make one T-shirt. *

257

Number of T-shirts worn at once: the record was set by Sanath Bandara (Sri Lanka) in Colombo, Sri Lanka, on December 22, 2011.

3,000

The number of band T-shirts owned by music fan Isac Walter.

6,000

The number of years cotton has been cultivated in Asia. *

23

The record for the most T-shirts folded in one minute, achieved by Graeme J. Cruden (UK) at a TK Maxx store in Manchester, United Kingdom, on March 3, 2009.

5½ MILES

Amount of cotton thread needed to make one T-shirt. *

1,320 GALLONS

Amount of water needed to make one T-shirt. *

N° 1

The United States is the biggest exporter of cotton (ahead of India). *

2

The T-shirt has two very famous siblings: the tank top and the polo shirt.

1860

The first woolen tank top.

1926

Appearance of the first polo shirt, worn by René Lacoste.

* Sources: *T-shirt stories* 2014 © Arte

THE T-SHIRT

IN THE BEGINNING

In the beginning was the cottonseed. So far, so unexciting, except that this almost miraculous seed would germinate into a true modern success story. How did the T-shirt transform over the course of the twentieth century from a simple utility garment to a mainstay of contemporary dress, a world best seller? Let's take a look at how it all began.

UNDERWEAR BECOMES OUTERWEAR

WHITE, BLACK, AND TANK TOP

The white T-shirt was originally a simple undergarment, before the sex symbols of the 1950s began boldly wearing it as regular outerwear, enshrining its iconic status among hunky rebels and trendy young things.

In the early twentieth century, the United States Navy issued its service personnel with a T-shaped, short-sleeved top made of white cotton that they could wear beneath their uniforms to make the latter more comfortable. This "T-shirt" was then issued to GIs during World War II. But it was Hollywood that made the immaculate white T-shirt truly popular. In 1951, *A Streetcar Named Desire* immortalized Marlon Brando, with his devastating pout, his dark gaze, and, of course, his white T-shirt, a symbol of an unbridled virility and a disquieting charm. The cut of the garment accentuated his muscular figure and tight torso, while the color highlighted the streaks of sweat of Brando at the height of his sex appeal. James Dean took things further in *Rebel Without a Cause* (1955), making the garment an emblem of sensual, rebellious youth. The success of the white T-shirt was now assured. It was adopted by hippies in the 1960s, while the grunge scene of the 1990s adored its "no logo" appeal, as did the "normcore" wave of the 2010s. The white T-shirt is a fashion statement in its own right. And as basic as it is, two other classic garments hang beside it in the everyday wardrobe: its dark doppelgänger, the black T-shirt, and its younger sibling, the tank top.

THE SEXIEST T-SHIRT EVER
1951: Marlon Brando, in *A Streetcar Named Desire*, made the white T-shirt the sexiest garment of its generation; the actor's bulging muscles and streaks of sweat heralded the dawn of an erotic revolution.

PRINT

Left: In 1942, American soldiers invented the printed T-shirt by customizing the white T-shirt issued to them as underwear.

Right: Named Miss Torpedo 1952 by The Torpedo Gang of the destroyer USS Henley, Marilyn Monroe posed in a T-shirt featuring their printed design.

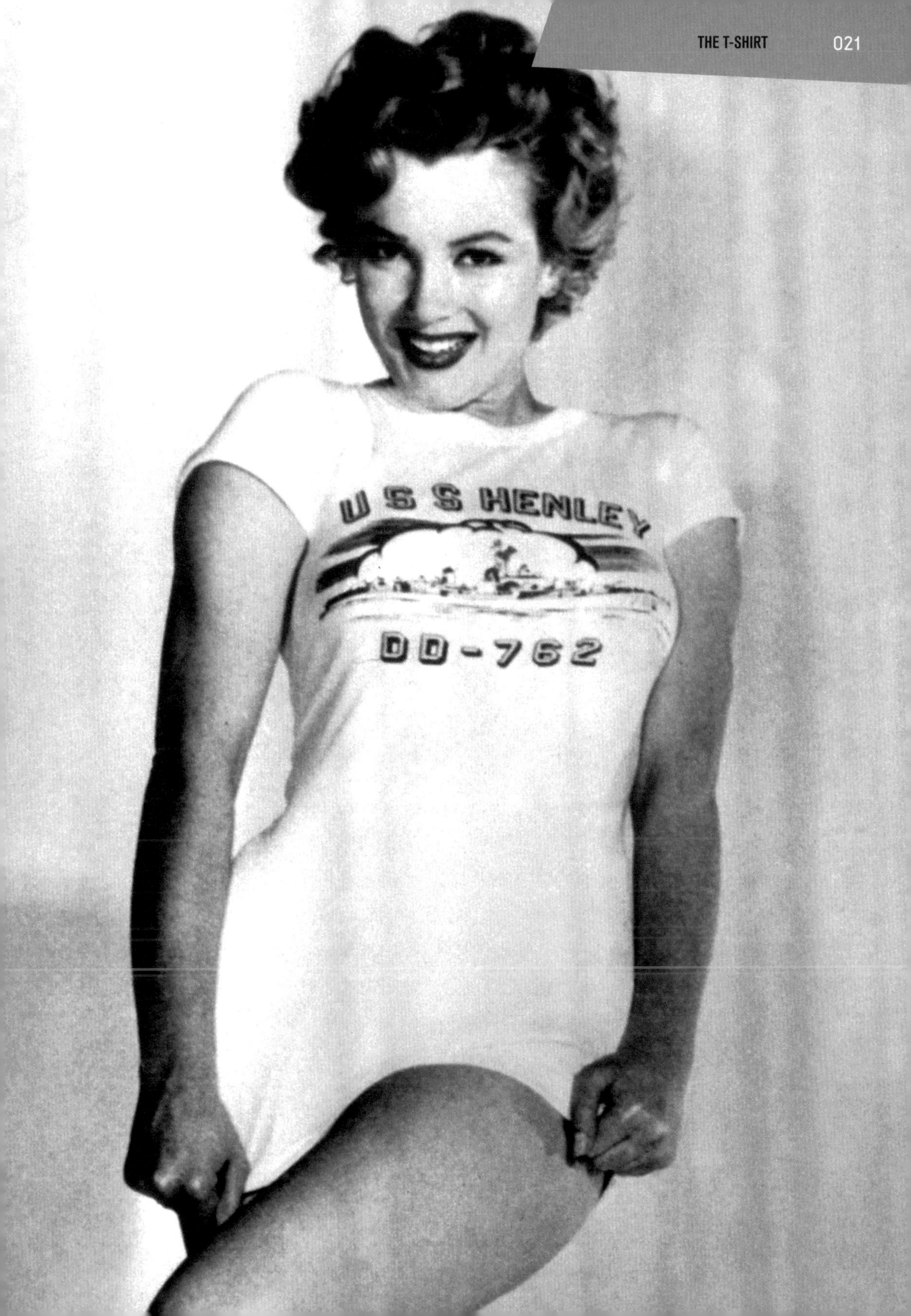
U S S HENLEY
DD-762

FRUIT OF THE LOOM
Historic brand, in white

FRUIT OF THE LOOM
Historic brand, in black

EMPORIO ARMANI
Italian luxury

PETIT BATEAU
The French touch, in white

PETIT BATEAU
The French touch, in black

BENETTON
Italian basic

A.P.C.
Minimalist French, in white

A.P.C.
Minimalist French, in black

CALVIN KLEIN
American giant

THE ROW
White tank top

HELMUT LANG
Black tank top

EQUIPMENT
Sleeveless T-shirt

CHLOÉ
Pastel tank top

ISABEL MARANT
Gray tank top

MARNI
Turtleneck

RAG & BONE
Flecked tank top

NIKE
Sporty tank top

ADIDAS
Sporty sleeveless T-shirt

THE BIG
T-SHIRT BRANDS

These are the brands that have helped make the T-shirt an essential garment. These institutions of the fashion world are all specialists in cotton T-shirts. They've spent many years redesigning and reinventing them each season. Their strength lies in the classic models on which their success and reputation are built.

FRUIT OF THE LOOM
The cult fruity logo

BENETTON
A redesigned logo

GAP
Three letters suffice

ABERCROMBIE & FITCH
The famous moose

A.P.C.
From Paris

EMPORIO ARMANI
EA7, the sporty brand

PETIT BATEAU
Original logo

PETIT BATEAU
"Les Escales Petit Bateau" collection
by Konbini

PETIT BATEAU
So chic

CALVIN KLEIN
The famous initials

CALVIN KLEIN
CK stylized

CALVIN KLEIN
CK trompe l'oeil

AMERICAN APPAREL
Stars and Stripes

AMERICAN APPAREL
Collaboration with artist
Charlie White III

AMERICAN APPAREL
Collaboration with artist
Charlie White III

AMERICAN APPAREL
100% MADE IN
LOS ANGELES

American Apparel may have been founded in Canada, but it remains one of the best-known American brands in the world. And it all started with T-shirts.

In 1989, Dov Charney founded a textile company in Montreal with a name that was anything but Quebecois: American Apparel. The entrepreneur then moved to South Carolina, where he began producing basic T-shirts, which he sold to silkscreen printers and wholesalers. In 1997, he moved production to California, with fifty employees (4,500 today). In 2003 American Apparel opened three boutiques, in Los Angeles, Montreal, and New York, and diversified its production. There was no logo, just a discreet poster campaign and a simple style that was popular with young people. Charney declared that American Apparel was a "heritage brand. It's like liberty, property, pursuit of happiness [...] That's my America." The company stands out because of its vertical integration. Everything happens in Los Angeles. The brand has a pro-immigrant policy and supports the LGBT cause, with its Legalize LA and Legalize Gay campaigns displaying true social investments. The AA factory is also ecologically responsible (reduced carbon footprint, use of solar panels). But the often provocative brand has also raised controversy, particularly with regard to its advertising: suggestive poses, porn actresses, and use of minors. Things turned sour for Charney in 2014, when he was sued for sexual harassment by his employees and models and lost control of the company. In 2015, American Apparel filed for bankruptcy before being taken over by several investment firms. It was the end for Charney, but not for the brand.

AMERICAN ADS
A key factor in American Apparel being able to win over the youth market was its highly natural advertisements. And what was so special about these images that got it so right? Nonprofessional models, who were often employees of the brand.

www.americanapparel.net

American Apparel®

MADE IN L.A.

Dov Charney founded American Apparel in Canada in 1989 before moving the company to Los Angeles. The brand prides itself on making 100 percent of its garments in California, and produces its iconic T-shirt in a range of colors that match the Pantone Matching System (on this page, PMS 1817 U, also known as Truffle). Despite a number of controversies linked to its sometimes provocative advertising and a dip in and out of bankruptcy in 2015, the brand's stores continue to offer the essence of AA: cool basics and a style that is American through and through.

OATMEAL
PMS 727 U

PALE YELLOW
PMS 7499 U

SORBET JERSEY
PMS 713 U

GOLD
PMS 122 U

SUN FIRE
PMS 172 U

PALE MAUVE
PMS 503 U

FUSCHIA
PMS 225 U

POPPY
PMS Red 032 U

BALLOON RED
PMS 1795 U

ULTRAVIOLET
PMS 2587 U

MENTHE
PMS 7457 U

GRASS
PMS 361 U

EMERALD
PMS 355 U

FOREST
PMS 330 U

OLIVE
PMS 371 U

SEA FOAM
PMS 5523 U

MERMAID GREEN
PMS 3135 U

BLUEBERRY
PMS 301 U

AMERICAN BLUE
PMS 289 U

ASPHALT
PMS 432 U

SILVER
PMS Cool Grey 2 U

BOOTCAMP GREY
PMS Cool Grey 4 U

SWAMP GREY
PMS 605 U

ASH GREY
PMS 5315 U

BROWN
PMS 476 U

PRINTS WITH RHYTHM

Music and T-shirts: an eternal love story. Musicians, bands, albums, and songs have always been printed, glorified, and immortalized on T-shirts. Pop, rock, punk, and rap, legendary artists or ephemeral boy bands, teen pop or heavy metal—without exception, all have had their own T-shirts, worn like a battle standard, and some of them conserved like precious relics.

SHADOWS AND LIGHT

ROCK AND HARD ROCK

The Rolling Stones, the Clash, the Sex Pistols, and Pink Floyd—these bands and everyone else all wore T-shirts, as did their fans. Thousands of different ones were produced throughout the 1960s and 1970s, with no self-respecting rocker being seen without one. A combination of advertising tool and badge of identity, the T-shirt is part and parcel of rock music.

Who has never worn the T-shirt of their favorite band? Beginning in the 1960s, rockers used T-shirts to make a special connection with their fans. A prime form of advertising, the T-shirt was merely a cotton flyer worn by rock fans as an emblem. On the front would be the band's name and often an album cover or a depiction of the band members. On the back would be information related to the band's current tour (dates, locations, etc.). T-shirts were generally bought on the way in (or out of) the gig, providing a not inconsiderable source of revenue for the bands, particularly those just starting out. But what was just a promotional tool very soon turned into a real sign of belonging, with fans proclaiming their love for their favorite band as they would a political message. The T-shirt is a garment with a voice. With a rebellious nod to this unstoppable trend, Johnny Rotten of the Sex Pistols shamelessly sported a T-shirt declaring, loud and clear, "I hate Pink Floyd."

THE SEX PISTOLS VS PINK FLOYD
Paul Cook, the drummer of the Sex Pistols, wears a T-shirt proclaiming his hatred of Pink Floyd. What did he dislike about them? Their pretension. Recently Johnny Rotten, lead singer of the Sex Pistols, who also wore the infamous T-shirt, revealed that he actually quite likes their early stuff, and even nicknamed his pet hamster after Pink Floyd founding member Syd Barrett.

THE CLASH
London Calling, 1979
The punk rock band's third album

THE CLASH
New York gigs, 1981

THE CLASH
"White Riot" in Notting Hill, London, 1977

THE WHO
Legendary Mod logo

THE WHO
Flamboyant US tour, 1979

THE WHO
Famous gig at the Goldhawk Club, London, 1965

THE RAMONES
Logo of the New York punk band

THE RAMONES
Punk USA

THE RAMONES
Ramones, the cult album of 1976

PINK FLOYD
The Dark Side of the Moon, 1973
The psychedelic band's eighth album

PINK FLOYD
Wish You Were Here, 1975
Reflective ninth album

KISS
Creatures of the Night, 1982
Tenth album by the face-painted rockers

KISS
Rock and Roll Over, 1976
A psychedelic design for the fifth album

LED ZEPPELIN
North American tour, 1975

LED ZEPPELIN
Magical concert at Wembley,
London, 1971

QUEEN
Symbolic logo for the royal rockers

QUEEN
Freddie Mercury and his group

RAGE AGAINST THE MACHINE
Raised fist for the political rockers

NIRVANA
Smiley face for the grunge rockers

NIRVANA
Nevermind

THE STOOGES
Chaotic gigs for acrobatic rockers

THE STOOGES
Iggy and his band

THE POLICE
Deadly trio

THE POLICE
Outlandos d'Amour, 1978
The first album

DAVID BOWIE
Aladdin Sane, 1973
Schizophrenic alien

DAVID BOWIE
Slick Starman

DAVID BOWIE
Thrilling world tour, 1972

THE CURE
Goth ambiance for rockers
in black and white

THE CURE
Robert Smith, enigmatic lead singer

SANTANA
Lotus flower

BRUCE SPRINGSTEEN
Born in the USA, 1984

BRUCE SPRINGSTEEN
Wrecking Ball, 2012

JIMI HENDRIX
Guitar hero

JIMI HENDRIX
Iconic

THE DOORS
Californian rockers

THE DOORS
The magnificent Jim Morrison

THE ROLLING STONES

The Rolling Stones have been producing official band T-shirts for nearly as long as they've been around. The instantly recognizable red tongue and lips logo (which first appeared in 1971, on the *Sticky Fingers* album) graces many of them. Little trophies for loyal fans, these T-shirts, particularly those designed for the band's tours, are now collector's items, sometimes handed down from generation to generation.

EUROPE
1967

UNITED KINGDOM
1969

UNITED STATES
1975

UNITED STATES
1978

UNITED STATES
1981

NORTH AMERICA
1989

BELGIUM
2014

AUSTRIA
2014

SWEDEN
2014

ISRAEL
2014

AUSTRALIA
2014

AUSTRALIA
2014

NORWAY
2014

NEW ZEALAND
2014

NEW ZEALAND
2014

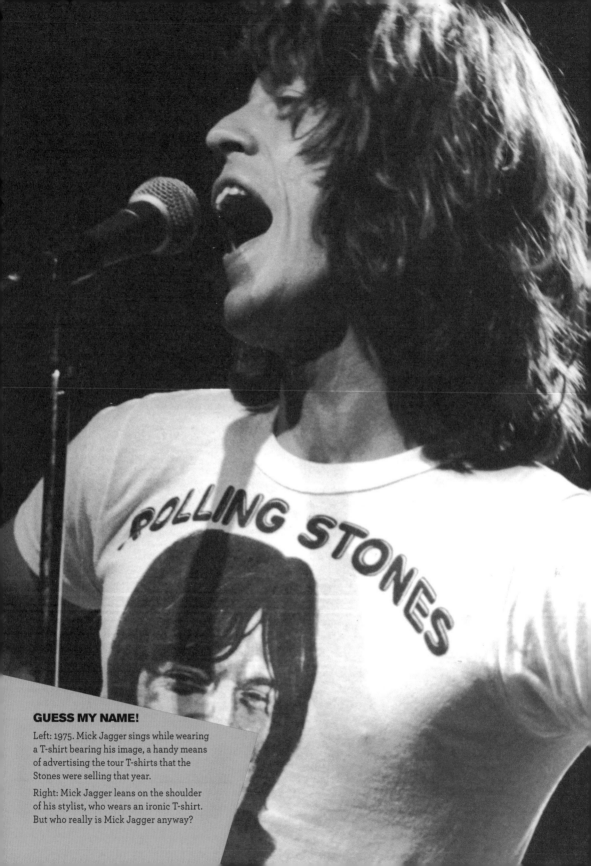

GUESS MY NAME!

Left: 1975. Mick Jagger sings while wearing a T-shirt bearing his image, a handy means of advertising the tour T-shirts that the Stones were selling that year.

Right: Mick Jagger leans on the shoulder of his stylist, who wears an ironic T-shirt. But who really is Mick Jagger anyway?

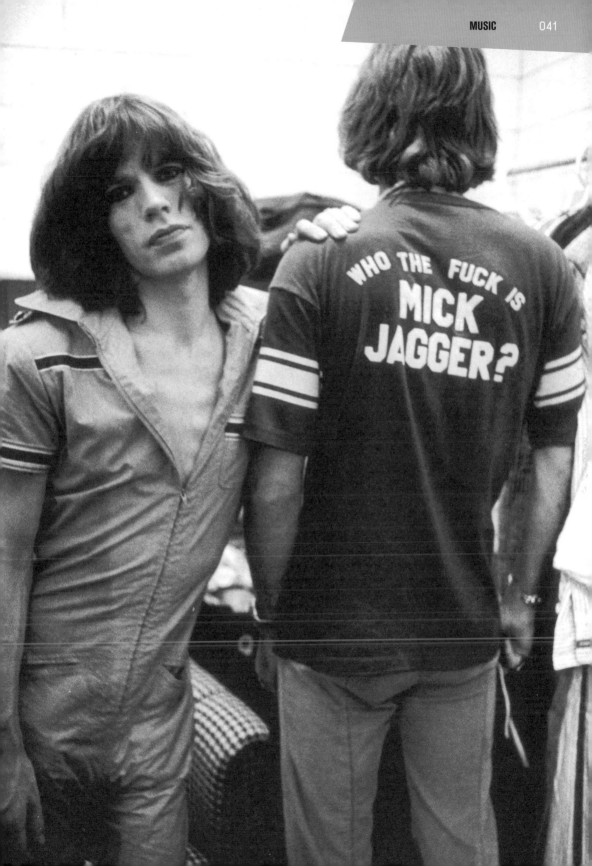

PUNK IS NOT DEAD !

It was the punks who turned the T-shirt into a real fashion item. It was very cheap and very easy to customize. Torn, stapled, pinned, ripped, and otherwise manipulated, the T-shirt became the manifesto of the "no future" generation. An emblem of the counterculture of the 1970s, the T-shirt was also the uniform of punk bands, starting with the Sex Pistols.

THE SEX PISTOLS
"Pretty Vacant," 1977

THE SEX PISTOLS
"God Save the Queen," 1977

THE SEX PISTOLS
"God Save the Queen," 1977

THE CASUALTIES
On the Front Line, 2004

JOY DIVISION
Unknown Pleasures, 1979

SIOUXSIE SIOUX
The feminine touch

NEVER MIND

THE BOLLOCKS

HERE'S THE

SeX PISTOLS

NEVER MIND THE BOLLOCKS, HERE'S THE SEX PISTOLS
In 1977, at the peak of the punk movement, the Sex Pistols released their one and only studio album, *Never Mind the Bollocks*, Here's the Sex Pistols, a record whose iconic cover caused a scandal, but which went to the top of the charts.

VIVIENNE WESTWOOD

PUNK PRINCESS

Vivienne Westwood is as essential to English fashion as the striped sailor's shirt is to French style. This designer and activist is as left field as she is talented, turning punk into a true art of living.

A teacher until the 1970s, this self-taught designer then sold jewelry, which she made herself, at Portobello Market. But it was her meeting with Malcolm McLaren that made the Westwood we all know. McLaren was the manager of the Sex Pistols, and he owned a clothing shop on King's Road called Let it Rock. Together they produced improbable clothes and renamed the shop SEX. The couple defined the aesthetics of punk fashion: do-it-yourself, repurpose, derision, and provocation of all kinds. Their designs were inspired by bikers, prostitutes, and fetishists. T-shirts, which Westwood and McLaren often wore, had pride of place in the wild punk wardrobe. They'd be ripped, stuck with safety pins, faded through repeat wash cycles, and covered with the most provocative symbols, such as the Nazi swastika or Christ on the cross. The aim? A social and cultural rant—something the designer would continue when her career became less underground. The Westwood style is unique: ethnic but not divisive, always punk, a bit provocative, and undeniably off the wall. The designer is a fervent supporter of Greenpeace, and has banned fur from her collections. She urges people to "buy nothing new," but adapt what they have, has made dresses from garbage bags, shaved her head to support ecologists, and has been married for over twenty years to a man twenty-five years her junior. Can't get more punk than that!

PUNK ATTITUDE
The tartan, the spiky haircut, the bone earrings, and the ripped, pinned, and overprinted T-shirt—all the paraphernalia of Vivienne Westwood, pictured here in the shop she opened with Malcolm McLaren.

COMPLETELY DESTROY

In the 1970s, Malcolm McLaren and Vivienne Westwood opened a shop on King's Road, in Chelsea, London, bearing the evocative name SEX. They sold fetish objects, leather and latex accessories, and provocative T-shirts, such as the famous Destroy model, which Westwood herself wore. In a particularly subversive touch, a large swastika was emblazoned on the chest and became a punk emblem.

ALICE IN PUNK LAND
Disney style

PUNK ARMY
At the ready

NO FUTURE
The Sex Pistols reference

KILL BONO
Antipop

PUNK IS NOT DEAD
Ultimate punk slogan

ANTI-FLAG
Apolitical

ANARCHY
Punk spirit

IN PUNK WE TRUST
Punk anthem

MUSIC KEEPS YOU UNDER CONTROL
By Vivienne Westwood and Malcolm McLaren

METALHEADS

Wailing guitars, headbanging, and ear-bleeding volume—these are just some of the things that heavy metal fans (and blues rock or American rock fans before them) want conveyed on the T-shirts of their favorite groups. These garments, which have achieved real fashion success, demonstrate a highly polished aesthetic, a mix of proud anarchism and dark romanticism. The only danger they face is that of becoming too mainstream, something their fans could never abide.

METALLICA
Metalheads since 1981

METALLICA
"Whiplash," 1983

METALLICA
"Seek & Destroy," 1983

AC/DC
"Hells Bells," 1980

AC/DC
"For Those About to Rock," 1981

AC/DC
Black Ice, 2008

GUNS N' ROSES, THE ROMANTICS
Given the band's name, it's not surprising that their imagery features both of these totemic items. The thorny roses are as hazardous as they are bewitching, while the guns signal brutality, the dark themes further emphasized by the skull. There is a clear inspiration from the kinds of tattoos that rockers often get.

IRON MAIDEN,
DEATH ROCKERS
Fantastical imagery,
devilish symbols,
characters who are
sometimes walking
dead (and usually
frightening),
lightning flashes,
explosions, and
hellfire—the T-shirts
of Iron Maiden fans
are as traumatizing
as the blistering
metal played
by the band.

GUNS N' ROSES
Skeletons, guns, and roses, since 1985

GUNS N' ROSES
Rarities: 1985–1994

IRON MAIDEN
"The Wicker Man," 2000

IRON MAIDEN
The Number of the Beast, 1982

SCORPIONS
German metal since 1965

SCORPIONS
Blackout, 1982

SCORPIONS
Return to Forever, 2015

BLACK SABBATH
Dark metal since 1968

BLACK SABBATH
Never Say Die! Tour, 1978

BLACK SABBATH
Mob Rules, 1981

DEEP PURPLE
Blues/rock/prog/metal since 1968

DEEP PURPLE
"Highway Star," 1972

DEEP PURPLE
Perfect Stranger, 1984

AEROSMITH
Glam metal since 1970

AEROSMITH
"Livin' on the Edge," 1993

ZZ TOP
Bearded blues rock since 1969

ZZ TOP
Texas metal since 1969

VAN HALEN
California metal since 1972

VAN HALEN
Tour of the World, 1984

JOAN JETT & THE BLACKHEARTS
Feminine hard rock since 1981

STYX
Paradise Theatre, 1981

GRATEFUL DEAD
Steal Your Face, 1976

GRATEFUL DEAD
Eclectic rock since 1965

POISON
"Cry Tough," 1986

ALICE COOPER
Shock rock since 1971

ALICE COOPER
Metal Medusa in 1971

ALICE COOPER
Madhouse Rock Tour, 1979

GENERATION POP ROCK

The T-shirt is the pop product par excellence, thanks to its accessibility and the way it brings people together. So what better than a T-shirt to promote loud and clear the most famous pop rock artists on the planet? From Michael Jackson to Madonna, by way of Coldplay, the whole of the "pop-sphere" find themselves on T-shirts.

MADONNA
Like a Virgin, 1984

MADONNA
Blond Ambition Tour, 1990

MADONNA
The MDNA Tour, 2012

PRINCE
Purple popster

PRINCE
"When Doves Cry"

PRINCE
Purple Rain, 1984

SUPERTRAMP
Breakfast in America, 1979

SUPERTRAMP
The Very Best of, 1974–1985

SUPERTRAMP
Crime of the Century, 1974

ELTON JOHN
Goodbye Yellow Brick Road, 1973

ELTON JOHN AND BILLY JOEL
Pop duo

BON JOVI
Romantic logo

BON JOVI
Slippery When Wet, 1986

DURAN DURAN
New wave icons

DURAN DURAN
Simon Le Bon, the lead singer

MICHAEL JACKSON
The myth

MICHAEL JACKSON
Thriller, 1982

MICHAEL JACKSON
Bad, 1987

MICHAEL JACKSON
Eternal silhouette

MICHAEL JACKSON
Moonwalker

NEW KIDS ON THE BLOCK
Five boys made in the 1980s

NEW KIDS ON THE BLOCK
Magic Summer Tour, 1990

THE BEACH BOYS
Surfin' USA, 1963

THE BEACH BOYS
Smile, 1966-1967

MUSE
Black Holes and Revelations, 2006

MUSE
Bold logo

COLDPLAY
Magic, 2014

COLDPLAY
X&Y, 2005

U2
The Best of, 1980-1990

U2
Irish ambassadors

BLUR
The Best of, 2000

PLACEBO
Meds, 2006

RADIOHEAD
Teddy bear logo

THE LEGENDARY BEATLES

There must be hundreds of thousands of T-shirts in the closets of Beatles fans across the globe, as each new generation discovers the "Fab Four," recalling a time when the lads from Liverpool set the benchmark for pop music. Each T-shirt is a dose of rock and nostalgia.

TWIST AND SHOUT
1964

A HARD DAY'S NIGHT
1964

A HARD DAY'S NIGHT
1964

STARS AND STRIPES TOUR
1964 and 1965

HELP
1965

HELP
1965

"TICKET TO RIDE"
1965

SERGEANT PEPPER'S LONELY
HEARTS CLUB BAND
1967

SERGEANT PEPPER'S LONELY
HEARTS CLUB BAND
1967

WHITE ALBUM
1968

YELLOW SUBMARINE
1969

YELLOW SUBMARINE
1969

"COME TOGETHER"
1969

LET IT BE
1970

APPLE RECORDS
The Beatles' label

HIP-HOP AND R&B: STREET CREDIBILITY

Rock doesn't have the monopoly of the T-shirt. Rap and R&B have also made much use of this easy means of promoting artists while affirming an aesthetic movement. Jay Z, 2Pac, 50 Cent, and Dr. Dre appear on T-shirts that have become true symbols of street culture, and their credo of slick, flowing rhymes with a touch of megalomania are evidenced by these T-shirts.

THE BEASTIE BOYS
Old School

RUN-D.M.C.
Made in Queens

WU-TANG CLAN
From Staten Island

DEATH ROW RECORDS
Legendary label

SNOOP DOGG
California rhymes

DR. DRE
Cult status

EMINEM
Straight outta 8 Mile

50 CENT
Mug shot

JAY Z
Legendary symbol

2PAC/NOTORIOUS B.I.G.
East Coast vs West Coast

2PAC
Martyr

JAY Z
Mogul

DESTINY'S CHILD
R&B girl group

MISSY ELLIOT
Hip-hop queen

RIHANNA
Provocation

1990S ALLURE

Left: Rapper Eminem wears an XXL white T-shirt during a gig in Los Angeles in 2006.

Right: Wyclef Jean, Lauryn Hill, and Pras of the Fugees decked out 1990s style with overalls, baseball cap, polo shirt, and, of course, T-shirts.

THE BEYONCÉ PHENOMENON

Millions of records sold, a shower of Grammy Awards, sexy moves to take your breath away, concerts that sell out in seconds, and a ton of T-shirts available online—Beyoncé is more than a recording artist. Each of her albums is a global event, with every music video garnering millions of hits, while her influence on the music industry continues to grow. There's a very special buzz around "Queen Bee."

FOR THE EMULATORS

FOR SHAKESPEARE LOVERS

FOR THE STRESSED

FOR THE FAITHFUL

FOR THE LIARS

FOR THE VEGANS

FOR THE PERFECTIONISTS

FOR BECKY

FOR THE DANCERS

FOR THE MUSTACHIOED

FOR THE ADMIRERS

FOR THE SPORTY

FOR THE SOLDIERS

FOR THE ARTISTS

FOR THE FEMINISTS

FESTIVALS

Music festivals are occasions for memorable musical experiences. The most legendary one is, of course, Woodstock, where the likes of Jimi Hendrix, Janis Joplin, Joe Cocker, and The Who performed. These days, there exists a musical festival for every musical genre. There's Corsica's Calvi on the Rocks for fans of electronica, or Hellfest for metalheads. And obviously each has its own T-shirt.

GLASTONBURY FESTIVAL
Muddy times

HELLFEST
Hard and heavy

SOLIDAYS
For good causes

LES FRANCOFOLIES
French focus

GOVERNORS BALL
New York's own

CALVI ON THE ROCKS
Sunny tunes

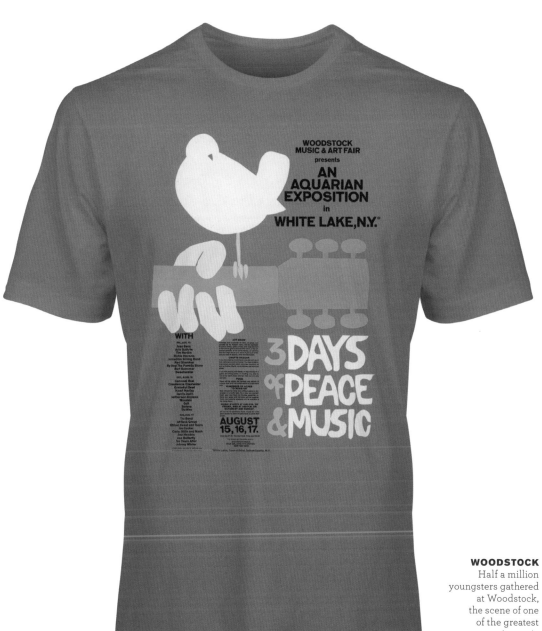

WOODSTOCK
Half a million youngsters gathered at Woodstock, the scene of one of the greatest moments in music history, for three days of "peace and music" (essentially pop, rock, and folk). The last hurrah of the hippie 1960s.

SÓNAR
Pure electronica

WEATHER FESTIVAL
Paris vibes

WE LOVE GREEN
Eco-friendly

ROCK IN RIO
International rock

EXIT FESTIVAL
Balkan beats

OUTLOOK FESTIVAL
Croatian grooves

LATITUDE FESTIVAL
Rural rhythms

FUJI ROCK FESTIVAL
Biggest fest in Japan

KAZANTIP
Beach party

ISLE OF WIGHT FESTIVAL

Located on the Isle of Wight, the eponymous pop festival is a little bastion of hippiedom. The first festival took place in 1968, and since then it has enjoyed a rather psychedelic image. The acts are now rather more mainstream, but the fans are no less dedicated.

HEAD HIGH, FIST RAISED

It's good to have convictions, and even better to display them. The activist T-shirt makes this possible, proving that fashion is an excellent vector of ideas. Whether supporting an electoral candidate, promoting a political, social, or cultural cause, or even triggering an international polemic, the T-shirt is always a good way to make one's opinions known.

T-SHIRT
FOR AN ELECTORAL CAMPAIGN:
THE WINNING TICKET

A presidential election sometimes hangs by a (cotton) thread, a tradition that began in the United States.

The first T-shirt intended to promote a presidential candidacy for the White House appeared in 1948. Thomas E. Dewey was the Republican governor of New York, and his face was printed on hundreds of white T-shirts, long before the practice became commonplace. His face was accompanied by the slogan "Dew it with Dewey," a play on words that, as striking as it was, failed to win him the election against Harry S. Truman. In 1952, Dwight Eisenhower's supporters wore a T-shirt with an equally well-remembered slogan, "I like Ike". The custom fell somewhat out of favor in the 1950s, before returning in a quite original manner in the late 1960s. In 1966, the Scott Paper Company decided to promote its toilet paper by offering housewives a dress made of paper for the modest sum of one dollar. This marketing ploy met with unexpected success. Intrigued, some political advisors decided to print the names and campaign slogans of presidential candidates on it. It wasn't long before the T-shirt began to be used for the same purpose. Trendier and more unisex than a dress, it was used by candidates of all persuasions, and has since become an essential element of any political campaign. Every candidate has his or her own T-shirt. Among the most recent to have truly struck a chord are the Hope T-shirt designed by Shepard Fairey for Barack Obama, and one designed by Marc Jacobs for Hillary Clinton, as well as the hipster-styled one promoting Bernie Sanders.

DARRYL "D.M.C." MCDANIELS
Rock the Vote is an organization that has been encouraging young people to vote since 1990, using cool imagery and cultural icons. For every US presidential campaign, thousands of people wear the official T-shirts of their chosen political party, including many celebrities who willingly lend their support. Here we see the singer of Run-D.M.C. at a fundraising concert.

SHEPARD FAIREY
FROM STREET ART TO POLITICS

It's one of the best-known posters in the world. And it was one of the most worn T-shirts of 2008. Shepard Fairey's "Hope" is undoubtedly part of history.

It all started with a poster. In the late 2000s, the artist Shepard Fairey was already known in the small world of street art for his visual "André the Giant has a Posse," a private joke among skaters. But it was the presidential campaign of 2008 that brought him unprecedented fame. The face of Barack Obama in red, white, and blue above the word "Hope" in capital letters would become the symbol of a renewal, for America and for the world. A host of flyers and posters soon followed, and the image was used in many different ways. The words "Change," "Vote," and "Progress" also appeared. A miracle of political marketing, the visual ended up on T-shirts that would become banners for Obama supporters throughout the campaign, led by many celebrities, including Beyoncé, Puff Daddy, Spike Lee, and Pierce Brosnan. The success was such that several magazines made it their cover, leading the very liberal *New Yorker* to say that Fairey's portrait was the most effective political illustration since the Uncle Sam "I Want You For US Army." Once elected, Obama sent Fairey a note with his thanks. Ultimate proof of the triumph—nearly ten years later, and despite the artist himself declaring Obama's presidency to have been rather disappointing, one can still buy the T-shirt online.

NEW HOPE
Shepard Fairey's Hope T-shirt depicting Barack Obama is not just a campaign T-shirt. It represents the fact that in 2008 an African-American man could aspire to the highest office in the land. A wonderful symbol.

REPUBLICAN PARTY
The official symbol: an elephant

DWIGHT D. EISENHOWER, REPUBLICAN
When the nickname is the slogan, 1952

RICHARD NIXON, REPUBLICAN
Pre-Watergate, 1972

RONALD REAGAN, REPUBLICAN
Let's Make America Great Again, 1980

**RONALD REAGAN AND
GEORGE H. W. BUSH, REPUBLICANS**
Winning ticket, 1980

GEORGE W. BUSH, REPUBLICAN
Forty-third president of the United States

DONALD TRUMP, REPUBLICAN
Make America Great Again, 2016 version

DONALD TRUMP, REPUBLICAN
US Veterans for Trump, 2016

DEMOCRACY
Rock the vote!

DEMOCRATIC PARTY
Official logo

JOHN F. KENNEDY, DEMOCRAT
The legend, 1960

JOHN F. KENNEDY, DEMOCRAT
President of renewal, 1960

BILL CLINTON AND AL GORE, DEMOCRATS
Dynamic duo, 1992

BARACK OBAMA, DEMOCRAT
Yes We Can, 2008

BARACK OBAMA, DEMOCRAT
Obama fever, 2008

HILLARY CLINTON, DEMOCRAT
For a woman president, 2016

HILLARY CLINTON, DEMOCRAT
Hill Yes! 2016

BERNIE SANDERS, DEMOCRAT
Candidate of the young generation, 2016

CHE GUEVARA
AN IMAGE
FOR ETERNITY

Ernesto "Che" Guevara is known all over the world, as is this famous image of him, Guerrillero Heroico, by photographer Alberto Korda. Gazing into the distance, his stately bearing has inspired generations of revolutionaries. An icon.

Havana, 1960. Che Guevara attends the funeral of the victims of the explosion of the French freighter *La Coubre*—an explosion that Cuba blamed on the CIA, accusing the United States of wanting to damage trade relations with Europe. During the memorial, Fidel Castro's photographer, Alberto Korda, took two photographs of the *Comandante*, immortalizing him. The portrait, *Guerrillero Heroico*, would become known around the world. Its first use dates from 1961, illustrating an article about Che in the magazine *Revolución*. Upon Guevara's death in 1967, the image was reproduced everywhere, as an ultimate symbol of the poetic hero, the romantic revolutionary. Korda tolerated all uses of the image, and gave a print to the Italian publisher Giangiacomo Feltrinelli. Thanks to a legal loophole— copyright wasn't recognized under Cuban law, since Fidel Castro considered it a "bourgeois concept"—Feltrinelli had one million copies printed. It became a cult image. In 1968, the Irish artist Jim Fitzpatrick created a stylized version of the image (emphasizing Che's features) on a red background. It is this image that has found itself printed on numerous T-shirts worn by generations of activists more or less familiar with the story of Guevara. Although he always declared that he supported the use of his photograph to pay homage to Che and his heritage, Korda did sue the vodka brand Smirnoff for using the image. *Viva la revolución*, not marketing!

QUE VIVA EL CHE!
A dark, penetrating gaze will remain etched in the collective memory as the symbol of Ernesto "Che" Guevara's struggle, thanks, largely, to the reproduction of a cult image on thousands of T-shirts across the world.

TO EACH THEIR CAUSE, TO EACH THEIR T-SHIRT

A T-shirt for a cause is a powerful thing, and it works. The greatest social struggles have often been immortalized on T-shirts, be it standing against violence, supporting victims of terrorist attacks, or promoting a religion. Some T-shirts become world-famous and go down in history when worn at demonstrations that are given massive media coverage.

WISE
Peace between the major world religions

PEACE AND LOVE
The universal peace symbol

ANTIWAR
A peace dove to stop war

DREAMER
John Lennon's "Imagine," a song for world peace

LIBERTY, EQUALITY, FRATERNITY
Motto of the French Republic

REBEL
For nonconformists

9/11
Homage to the victims of the terrorist
attacks of September 11, 2001

JOURNALISTS
Message in support of the *Charlie Hebdo* staff
murdered in Paris on January 7, 2015

PARIS
Message in support of those killed in the
Paris attacks of November 13, 2015

SPAIN
Spanish political slogan against fascism

TIBET
Message in support of Tibetan independence,
drawn by the French artist Ben

PALESTINE
Palestine liberation movement

UNIVERSALIST
For a world without borders

WELCOMING
German movement to welcome refugees since
November 2014

ANARCHISM
Anarchist slogan

ANTI-RACIST
Not here!

ANTI-FASCIST
Design by French militant band
Kiddam and the People

DON'T TOUCH MY BUDDY
Slogan of French charity SOS Racisme since 1984

HISTORIC
Amnesty International, pioneering defender
of human rights

FAMILY VALUES
Slogan of the movement opposing
same-sex marriage in France

KIDS
The international NGO fighting for
children's rights since 1919

PRO-GAY
In support of legalizing gay marriage
in the United States

PRIDE
The rainbow flag,
symbol of LGBT pride

PRO-ANIMAL
PETA, protecting animals' rights
since 1980

WORKER
Something to be

DEMOCRACY
Where is it?

ANTICAPITALIST
For a new social order

ANARCHO-COMMUNISM
Radical revolution

ANTIDRUGS
Choose life!

CANNABISM
Promoting the legalization of cannabis consumption
in the United States

ANONYMOUS
A loose community of hackers working
anonymously in support of various causes

SKINHEADS
Nonconformist

PUSSY RIOT
Feminist Russian punk-rock group,
since 2011

GIRL POWER

The T-shirt is a wonderful tool for feminists to defend and promote women's rights, including equal pay, access to education, and freedom of expression or opinion. The subjects are varied, and each time the message hits the nail right on the head.

ABORTION
My body, my choice

ANTIPATRIARCHY
End of patriarchy

PINK PONY
Ralph Lauren against breast cancer

I TOUCH MYSELF
Campaign to encourage women
to check for signs of breast cancer

SEIN° LAURENT
Fashion homage by My Boobs Buddy,
a brand that fights against breast cancer

BATTLE ON
For fierce women

**SIMONE
DE BEAUVOIR**
Synonymous with
the women's
liberation
movement, this
feminist theorist and
goddess of French
intellectuals is also
famous for her
powerful words and
a certain kind of
tough romanticism.
A model
for girls today.

* *Sein* is the French word for "breast," but is pronounced the same way as Saint.

**STRONG ENOUGH
X BA&SH**
The designers
Barbara Boccara and
Sharon Krief have
been involved with
the Pink October
breast cancer
awareness campaign
since 2014. Their
contribution is a
T-shirt of which all
the profits go
to the charity.

ICONIC
Rosie the Riveter

FUNDAMENTAL
Cyndi Lauper revisited

FEMINIST HUMOR
Pizza, not pigeonholing!

LOGO
Girl power

FEEL THE FORCE
Strong women

DEFINITION
We can all be feminists

INDEPENDENT
One-woman fairy tale

ANTI-MISOGYNIST
Enough is enough

FLORAL FEMINIST
Soft power

I CAN'T BREATHE/HIV POSITIVE

Left: In 2014, Kobe Bryant protests against the death of Eric
Garner, an African-American man who died after being violently
arrested by the police in Staten Island. One of the police officers
placed Garner in a choke hold, after which Garner repeated the
words "I can't breathe" several times before falling unconscious.
He was pronounced dead at the hospital an hour later.

Right: Nelson Mandela visits AIDS victims in a hospital in the
township of Khayelitsha, South Africa. The former president
was always ready to publicize the fight against the disease.

POSITIVE

HIV
POSITIVE

H.I.V

POSITIVE

...arch for Access to Treatments for HIV/AIDS
Durban, South Africa July 2000

ISSUED BY TREATMENT ACTION CAMPAIGN (TAC)

WHEN T-SHIRTS
GO GREEN

A T-shirt is relatively environmentally friendly. It keeps for a long time, can be used over and over again, and dyed jet-black when we get bored with it. And if the cotton used to make it is organic, then all the better. Perfect for activists trying to reduce humanity's carbon footprint while promoting their favorite cause. Save trees, wear T-shirts.

WORLD WIDE FUND FOR NATURE
Protecting nature since 1961

NUCLEAR
Just say no

GMO
Protect our food

PLANET EARTH SPEAKS TO US
Listen to her

CLIMATE CHANGE
Not cool!

SAVE THE PLANET
We're all superheroes!

FUEL SUICIDE
Switch to renewables!

WHERE THERE ARE TREES . . .
. . . there's hope!

THINK GREEN
Tomorrow's energy

SAVE THE TREES
Go green!

VEGETARIAN
This guy was!

VEGAN
Sparing all animals

GREENPEACE
NGO since 1971

EARTH'S LUNGS
Save the forests

CYCLE
Recycle!

SMALL SCANDAL
OR MAJOR POLEMIC

A simple T-shirt can sometimes stir spirited debate. Social media can eagerly fan the flames of controversial T-shirts designed and/or worn by rabble-rousers returning to the punk tactic of using clothes to provoke. Fascist symbols, political scandals, and borderline messages—sometimes the scandal subsides as quickly as it flared up, after a good dose of publicity, of course.

BOY LONDON
The fashion brand's logo was heavily criticized for
its resemblance to a Nazi symbol

SCANDAL AT UEFA
Diego Maradona calls Michel Platini
and Sepp Blatter thieves

PARIS TERRORIST ATTACKS
A TV show hires an actor to wear this T-shirt in
order to analyze the reactions of passersby

URBAN OUTFITTERS
Symbol of one of the most dangerous gangs in
Chicago, the Gangster Disciples

ZARA
Zara prints a racist message
while trying to parody a fashion maxim

WHAT ABOUT YVES?
Hedi Slimane changes the name of the Yves Saint
Laurent brand by removing the "Yves," and inspires
a designer, who then runs into legal trouble

VAGINAL SCANDAL

American Apparel is used to facing scandals. In 2013, a quite explicit Period Power T-shirt featuring menstruation, hairiness, and masturbation caused a stir, particularly online. For the brand it was a feminist statement, for others it was a vulgar provocation.

IMPRISONED
FOR A T-SHIRT

Wearing a T-shirt can prove risky. In 2008, a young Lebanese man paid the price for wearing a Marc Jacobs T-shirt.

"Protect the skin you're in" was the message that Marc Jacobs printed on his T-shirts in the late 2000s to support the fight against skin cancer. And what illustration accompanied it? A star in her birthday suit: Irina Shayk, Kate Moss, Miley Cyrus, Naomi Campbell, Heidi Klum, or Victoria Beckham printed naked, but with breasts and genitals hidden, on T-shirts of all colors. The message was really clear. It was a cool T-shirt for a noble cause, the perfect combination to create a fashion must-have, and young people bought it in droves. Raffi Nernekian, a twenty-eight-year-old Lebanese man, bought one of the T-shirts in New York, which he then wore in Dubai, where he had been working for four years. One day when he was at a bakery, a hand clamped down on his arm: that of a man with a telephone. Nernekian heard him talking of a naked woman, an indecent T-shirt. The police arrived. After a fruitless attempt to settle the matter amicably, the young man was handcuffed and marched off to the police station. He was eventually sentenced to one month in prison and expelled from Dubai once he had served his time. But his freedom came at the price of six months of legal battles. In 2009, the United Arab Emirates reaffirmed the duty of foreign visitors to respect the local dress regulations, which stipulate that clothes must be decent. Nernekian declared, however, that the rules are unclear in Dubai and that he had already worn this T-shirt without any trouble. But a T-shirt sometimes can be more offensive than one thinks.

NAKED FOR A GOOD CAUSE
Here we see the English top model Cara Delevingne posing naked for Marc Jacobs in support of the fight against skin cancer.

BRANDED

As anyone who works in advertising knows all too well, the T-shirt is an excellent promotional tool. It is both practical and cheap, and can turn any human being into a sandwich board. One finds all kinds on T-shirts, from simple brand names to rousing slogans and slick advertisements. And there is no shortage of parodies and twists on these. In fact, the flow seems to be endless.

A NOW LEGENDARY LOGO

"I love New York." It's so simple it might never have seen the light of day. And yet this minimalist message and logo have become one of the most famous emblems of the city that never sleeps.

In 1977, New York was experiencing a drop in popularity. Dirty streets, high crime rates, and a general feeling of insecurity had tarnished the image of the Big Apple. The state authorities decided to invest in an advertising campaign that would kickstart a dialogue between the city and its inhabitants, as well as attracting tourists, to make New York an essential destination. The commission went to Milton Glaser, the art director of the advertising agency chosen for the project. And what was his masterstroke? Three black letters, in the American Typewriter typeface, framing a red heart. A clear, concise, and strong message: "I love New York." It was very much in line with Glaser's design philosophy of seeking simplicity at all costs, in order to achieve something that looks like it was the only possible solution to the brief. The logo very quickly found itself on a simple white T-shirt. It was a triumph. The T-shirts sold by the thousand and became a must-have item to bring back from a trip to New York. The campaign was never meant to last more than a few weeks, and yet the T-shirts are still being sold all over the city forty years later. Glaser gave his rights to the logo to New York for free, never expecting it to become the commercial success that it has been.

I LOVE NEW YORK AND ELSEWHERE
So huge is the phenomenon that riffs on the original can be found on T-shirts across the globe. Go to any souvenir shop or kiosk and you'll find a T-shirt with the red heart boasting love for the town in question.

NEW YORKER

BEARDY

IDOL

BLOODY

BRITISH

EGOCENTRIC

SMILEY

POETIC

DISNEY

KEEP CALM
AND CARRY ON

The original slogan was created by the British Ministry of Information in 1939 for use on a poster to raise the morale of the population. Although 2.5 million were printed, only a handful were actually used. It was not until 2000 that a bookstore owner found a copy in a box of secondhand books he'd bought. Since then, this symbol of the British stiff upper lip has become immensely popular, inspiring all kinds of weird and wacky variants, and printed on all sorts of objects, including T-shirts, of course.

ORIGINAL

ZOMBIES

RUGBY

DANCE

PARTY

ROCK

READING

OSTEOPATHY

NINJA TURTLES

SUPERHERO

THE LION KING

SHOPPING

BOBBY MCFERRIN

HUGS

E.T.

LOGOMANIA

What better form of publicity can there be than clearly displaying one's logo? This easily recognizable symbol, the heart of a brand's visual identity, enjoys extreme marketing power. In the 1990s, it became very trendy to put it on a T-shirt, as well as on sportswear and even garments produced by top luxury brands. The vogue faded with the dawn of the 2000s, but there has been a resurgence in recent years.

CHUPA CHUPS
"The Pleasure of Sucking"

PEPSI
"The Choice of a New Generation"

SPRITE
"Obey Your Thirst"

COCA-COLA
"Taste the Feeling"

BURGER KING
"Have It Your Way"

NESQUIK
"You Can't Drink It Slow"

MCT-SHIRT

McDonald's Golden Arches, designed in 1962, are ubiquitous. They were, in fact, inspired by two yellow arches that decorated the facade of the chain's very first restaurant. In 2009, the background became green in support of sustainable development.

STARBUCKS COFFEE
"Bring On the Day"

DICKIES
"We're Basic"

HARD ROCK CAFE
"Love All, Serve All"

DANONE
"Hmmm, Danone"

CAMEL
"Pleasure to Burn"

MARTINI
"No Martini, No Party"

HEINEKEN
"Open Your World"

RED BULL
"Red Bull Gives You Wings"

NO LOGO
Is silence golden?

VERSACE
Italian Medusa

VON DUTCH
Streetwear USA

ED HARDY
"Love Kills Slowly"

FENDI
Italian fur

PRADA
Italian legend

COMME DES GARÇONS
Japanese brand

BALMAIN
"New French Style"

LEVI'S
"Now Is Our Time"

LACOSTE
"Become What You Are"

ADIDAS
"Impossible is Nothing"

BIC
"You Probably Didn't Buy It"

LEGO
"Just Imagine . . ."

NASA
"To Reach for New Heights"

BMW
"The Ultimate Driving Machine"

CATERPILLAR
"Earthmoving Solutions For Today's Challenges"

GOOGLE
"Make the World a Better Place"

LIFE
A life in images

MTV
"You'll never look at music
the same way again"

THE ORIGINAL APPLE

The famous Apple logo was designed by Rob Janoff, who explained that the bite was included for scale and also to avoid confusion with a cherry. As for the rainbow stripes, he said, "the Apple II was the first home or personal computer that could reproduce images on the monitor in color. So it represents color bars on the screen. Also, it was an attempt to make the logo very accessible to everyone, especially to young people."

PRETTY PARODIES

Adapting a brand's logo, slogan, or more generally the fundamentals
of its visual identity is also a kind of promotion in itself. Some
of these T-shirts are amusing, others controversial, but they are
all forms of disguised advertising in spite of themselves.

ADIDAS
Exotic style

ADIDAS
For the addicts

PUMA
Star Wars style

NIKE
Ode to sausage

NIKE
Twitter fan

THE NORTH FACE
. . . of Kenny

LACOSTE
West Coast croc

LACOSTE
Cheapness

LEVI'S
Anagram

CÉLINE
Luxury singer

LOUIS VUITTON
Luxury Harry Potter

JACK DANIEL'S
The Nightmare Before Christmas

NTV
No television

LEGO
For the nerds

MONOPOLY
Brainless

PROMOTIONAL COUP

When a brand is going all out on the promotional front, the range of goodies usually includes a T-shirt, since it is easy to design, produce, and distribute, and people really love them. The most striking examples don't even include the brand name.

SPORTY BABY
Evian

COOL BABY
Evian

MUSICAL BABY
Evian

TEDDY BEAR
Haribo

TAGADA STRAWBERRY
Haribo

CROCODILES
Haribo

CRAZY BABIES
"Evian, live young," reads the advertisement. And what could be younger than a chubby baby who dances, laughs, roller skates, and listens to music through headphones clamped to its ears, like a real teenager? But the real stroke of genius of these T-shirts is to place the illustration so that the baby's neck meets the wearer's neck, creating a trompe l'œil effect. The advertising promises rejuvenation, and the T-shirt provides it.

DOUBLE CHEESE
McDonald's

HOT FUDGE SUNDAE
McDonald's

LARGE FRIES
McDonald's

MISS GREEN
M&M's

RED
M&M's

YELLOW
M&M's

OASIS
Pear

OASIS
Orange

OASIS
Mango

© 2013 Schweppes International Ltd.

GET FRUITY!
In the early 2010s, Oasis soft drinks got an original promotional treatment in France. A cool, funny, cheeky mascot was created for each fruit, with amusing slogans and slick, modern imagery. And there was an online store that sold T-shirts featuring the fun little characters.

SOUVENIRS

One of the most universal types of T-shirt is the one we bring back from a trip. It's the easiest souvenir for a sentimental tourist to find, and can serve either as a reminder of a pleasant holiday or as a gift for a friend or loved one back home. Some bear the name of a town, others a picturesque postcard or a stylized photograph, but all evoke the allure of travel.

ROCK ON NEW YORK!
New York City, New York

CALIFORNIA, HERE WE COME . . .
California

OKLAHOMA IS OK
Oklahoma

SWEET HOME CHICAGO
Chicago, Illinois

WELCOME TO MIAMI
Miami, Florida

ALOHA HAWAII!
Hawaii

BOM DIA RIO!
Rio de Janeiro, Brazil

¡HOLA ARGENTINA!
Argentina

¿QUÉ TAL MADRID?
Madrid, Spain

WET IN IBIZA
Ibiza, Spain

SWINGING LONDON
London, United Kingdom

ROMULUS AND REMUS
Rome, Italy

KALIMERA!
Mykonos, Greece

THE PYRAMIDS
Cairo, Egypt

ARIGATO TOKYO
Tokyo, Japan

**WHAT HAPPENS
IN VEGAS . . .**
. . . often fits on a
T-shirt. The city that
lights up Nevada is,
above all, a tourist
resort. With its
garish colors and
gaudy casinos, its
nickname fits like
a glove: Sin City!

TEXAS RODEO
Anyone wanting to bring back a souvenir of the Lone Star State can't go wrong with this vintage-looking T-shirt that evokes the very soul of Texas: a cowboy, with Stetson clamped to his head, flies across the landscape astride his galloping charger.

PARIS SPECIAL

With millions of tourists visiting each year, the most beautiful avenue in the world, and the Eiffel Tower's beam of light illuminating the city, Paris is a true treasure. It's a fashion capital, a cultural mecca, and favorite romantic destination. Unsurprising, then, that there are dozens of T-shirts paying homage to it. We love Paris.

TOURIST PARIS
Souvenirs de France

PARIS COAT OF ARMS
Petit Bateau

LEGENDARY PARIS
A.P.C.

PARIS THE CAPITAL
Levi's

PARIS NO LIMITS
Être Cécile

HELLO PARIS
Être Cécile

MADE IN PARIS
Commune de Paris 1871 is a designer label founded by two Parisians. It has been producing fashion items dedicated to the City of Light since 2009. The revolutionary soul of the Paris Commune is evoked by the choice of symbols and the energy of the design—a brand for Parisians who refuse to be beaten down.

PARIS SOCCER COLORS
L'Amicale du Ballon

PARIS BEACH
Boma Store Ferrara

PARIS PRINCE
Apadana

PARIS CANCAN
Atelier Amelot

PARIS TRIUMPHANT
Walk in Paris

NEARLY PARISIAN
Être Cécile

DEUTSCH PARISIEN
Civissum

PARIS NUMBER 1
Chauvin Paris

PARIS GIRL
Maison Kitsuné

PARIS DREAMER
Wildfox

PARIS DWELLER
Civissum

PARIS ACTIVIST
OBEY

PARIS TRUANT*
Extraball

PARIS VACATION
Faguo

PARIS INTO SPACE
Commune de Paris 1871

PARIS AND HER IRON LADY
Kenzo

PARIS BILINGUAL
Atelier Amelot

PARIS KISS
Florette Paquerette

* The French expression *faire l'école buisonnière* means "to play truant."

LET'S HEAR IT FOR NEW YORK!

The Big Apple is eternal. Legendary monuments, a unique skyline, a fabulous atmosphere, and everything that makes up New York's DNA can be found on T-shirts. Whether a souvenir for a die-hard tourist, or a proclamation of identity for a lifelong New Yorker, to each their own declaration of love for NYC.

STREETS OF NEW YORK
The iconic fire escape

NEW YORK CITY
Timeless T-shirt

SYMBOLIC NEW YORK
The Big Apple

SUPERMAN IN NEW YORK
Better than Metropolis

NYC
Says it all

NEW YORK . . .
. . . chooses its friends!

SPIDERMAN
Flatiron Building,
where Peter Parker works

NYC LADY
Statue of Liberty

UNBELIEVABLE NEW YORK
Empire State Building

ETERNAL NEW YORK
Manhattan skyline

NEW YORK NEVER SLEEPS
Particularly in Times Square

CENTRAL PARK
New York's oasis

TAXI!
Yellow and checks

DESTINATION:
New York

NEW YORK ISLANDS
Ferry tour

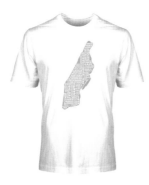

MANHATTAN
The legendary island

STATEN ISLAND
Borough of parks

GREENWICH VILLAGE
Sunday stroll

BROADWAY
On stage!

HARLEM
Uptown neighborhood

LITTLE ITALY
A taste of the Mediterranean

CHINATOWN
Exotic flavors

THE BRONX
Cradle of hip-hop

BROOKLYN
In the footsteps of Spike Lee

QUEENS
Largest borough

CONEY ISLAND
Trip to the funfair

BROOKLYN NETS
B-Ball in BK

NEW YORK RANGERS
For hockey fans

NEW YORK KNICKS
Support the team

NEW YORK JETS
Football fashion

NEW YORK GIANTS
For fans of the Big Blue

NEW YORK YANKEES
Since 1901

METS
Yankees' rivals

LATCHING ONTO A TREND

Some T-shirts meet with universal acclaim because they're able to cross borders and trigger feelings everyone can share, or because they represent a particular generation, a cultural practice, or a societal phenomenon. Everyone has either seen them, worn them, or bought them as gifts. These T-shirts unite people, for they express something of the "here and now."

WHEN A T-SHIRT GOES VIRAL . . .

. . . AND VICE VERSA

The Internet has an incredible capacity to exponentially magnify nearly any message. And it's fascinating to see the extent to which Internet buzz and a T-shirt can be closely linked, either because one promises the other, or because the latter is a means of capturing a phenomenon that would otherwise never have endured.

The perfect example of a T-shirt that could/should have remained forever hidden in the depths of the Internet, but which an absurd buzz transformed into a real phenomenon, is that of the Three Wolf Moon T-shirt in 2008. While searching for a textbook on Amazon.com, a student came across a product recommendation for this seemingly banal T-shirt. Amused by its kitsch (three wolves howling at a full moon), he posted a spoof review mentioning the supposedly supernatural powers of the T-shirt, including the ability to attract women. In no time at all, a host of other people also posted spoof reviews, each funnier than the next. The buzz then spread across various social media, and the T-shirt began to sell like hotcakes, especially when it became a hipster must-have item. As its popularity soared, this in turn boosted the original Internet buzz. An hour is an eternity on the web, and one buzz is soon swept aside by another in a torrent of posts, likes, and tweets. In a world 2.0 where the immediate is king, a T-shirt is an aide-mémoire. So what works best on a T-shirt? A meme, of course—that riffs on an existing image or phrase made famous by viral propagation, such as Grumpy Cat, the Ryan Gosling "Hey Girl," or the Dawson Crying meme, all of which have been immortalized on T-shirts.

THREE WOLVES AND A MOON
Magic? Perhaps a little bit, because these three wolves howling at the moon have attained cult status. A cheesy T-shirt of the kind that is usually the preserve of aging rockers attempting a comeback is now a hipster must-have. The magic of fashion!

UNICORN
Geek totem

UNICORN + RAINBOW = LOL
Geek equation

MY LITTLE UNICORN
Riff on the vintage toy

LOLOMGWTF
Internet ABC

JOKE 2.0
For ironic netizens

SO LITTLE TIME
For web addicts

DAVID HASSELHOFF
Most "vintage" meme

RYAN GOSLING
Sexiest meme

DAWSON
Weepiest meme

BRIGADE OF THE LOLCATS
Superheroes of the net

KITTEN OVERLOADS
The cheesier, the cooler

NYAN CAT
First lolcat on the net

GRUMPY CAT
David Bowie style

GRUMPY CAT
Kitty hates

GRUMPY CAT
No means no

GRUMPY CAT
Obama style

HIPSTER CAT
Hipster shades and hipster sky

SELF-REFERENTIAL
Lolcat goes LOL

CHEESY OR NOT . . .

Cheesy, kitschy, outdated, and old-fashioned—these T-shirts are all that and more, but they have nevertheless become trendy again. Hipster culture has placed T-shirts depicting a kitten, dolphins, and the Spice Girls center stage of the current fashion scene. The outmoded images and hokey themes somehow makes them even funnier.

**PINK LEOPARD PRINT
IS A SUPER COMBINATION**

**MAGICAL KINGDOM FOR
SERIOUS GEEKS**

BUCOLIC POSTCARD

MMMBOP!

**ROBIN WILLIAMS, KING OF THE
1990S**

SPICE UP YOUR LIFE!

GANG OF DOLPHINS

FREE WILLY?

GOLDEN EAGLE

AMERICAN STEED

WOLFPACK

EYE OF THE TIGER

KING OF THE HAMSTERS

CUTE KITTEN

SWEET LABRADOR

THE JOKE'S ON YOU!

T-shirts that play with illusions, often with hilarious results, have become very popular. It all began with the famous tuxedo T-shirt, ushering in a wave of trompe l'œil creations. From bikinis to bomber jackets and fake muscles, there is no shortage of amusing models.

FLORAL BIKINI AND BARBIE BODY

IN CLARK KENT MODE

INCOGNITO AT THE BEACH!

BLING BLING!

FOR TOUGH GUYS AND GALS

LUXURY LIFE VEST

SUPERCHIC
The tuxedo T-shirt was born in the United States in the 1960s, but it wasn't at all meant as a joke. It was even worn for weddings! Since then, it has become mainly a basic for Halloween costumes.

THE SMILEY
ONE CRAZY STORY

It's yellow, it smiles, and it has the power to put you in a good mood. The smiley is used by millions of people across the world every day. Here is its story.

Massachusetts, 1963. An insurance company commissions a freelance artist to create an image to raise the morale of its employees, who were down in the dumps after a rather complicated merger. Harvey Ball, who founded his design company in 1959, was given the brief. A yellow circle, two eyes, and a smile—it was so simple, but it won over the executives, who gave him forty-five dollars for this original creation. Badges were then handed out to the employees. It worked, and the "smiley" became a true icon. But since Ball had not registered the copyright of his design, the financial gain for him was tiny. Frenchman Franklin Loufrani avoided the same error when, in 1971, he placed the smiley on the pages of *France Soir*, the newspaper for which he worked. Loufrani registered the trademark of the logo and earned one centime for each of the twelve million stickers sold during that period. The success of the smiley was exponential, with all kinds of derivative products hitting the market: badges, shoes, jewelry, candy, car stickers, and, of course, T-shirts. These days, Nicolas Loufrani runs his dad's company, based in London. The family jealously guards its baby, suing anyone who dares to use the smiling yellow face without its authorization. Early on in his career, Franklin Loufrani is said to have told his wife, "I need to find a great idea to earn money." He must surely be smiling now.

SMILE!
The smiley has been parodied in many ways. In 1994, Robert Zemeckis attributed its creation to Forrest Gump (in the eponymous film), who wipes his muddy face on a T-shirt, leaving the imprint of two eyes and a smile.

GEEK CULTURE

The geeks of generation Y are not just excellent coders. Science,
technology, superheroes, video games, and sci-fi and heroic
fantasy series are part of their everyday entertainment.
And they love to display their passions and their geek culture
on their T-shirts.

SMILEY FACE
The first emoticon

GAME BOY
Vintage console

I'M THINKING . . .
Inside a geek's brain

SPACE INVADERS
Geek obsession since 1978

CALL OF DUTY
Gamers' choice

GODZILLA
Japanese monster and geek fave

ANGRY BIRDS
Favorite smartphone game

MARIO
The best-known plumber in the world

PEAR VS APPLE
Geek joke

THE BIG BANG THEORY
The geek series par excellence

CONTROL+ALT+DELETE
The solution to everything

POKÉMON
The 1990s phenomenon is back

ZELDA
Nintendo legend

LEGO
Timeless toy

RUBIK'S CUBE
Nerd challenge

PAC-MAN MANIA
Pac-Man was created in Japan in 1980 and would become a firm favorite with gamers of all ages. The principle is simple: a little yellow figure must eat all the pac-dots on a given map, while avoiding the various enemies, or "ghosts." There would be no shortage of successful games to come (Super Mario Bros., Zelda, and more), but Pac-Man remains seared into the collective memory.

ALL I KNOW
I LEARNED FROM COMICS

STAY UP LATE · STICK BY YOUR BRO · BE FLY · KEEP IT GREEN · GO FASTER

BUST A RHYME · SHOOT STRAIGHT · FLIP IT · GET PAID · ACT LIKE A BOSS

HOT GIRLS OWN · STOP CLOWNIN' · STRETCH IT OUT · GIRLS ARE CRAZY · SURF'S UP

GET WEIRD · ALIENS ARE REAL · HATERS GONNA HATE · READ A BOOK · BIRD IS THE WORD

SUPERHEROES FOR ALL
Why not learn from your favorite superheroes? Each one comes with a mini life lesson that's worth remembering, such as "Keep it green," "Stick by your bro," "Stay up late," and "Get weird." So true and so funny.

WONDER WOMAN
Superheroine

WONDER WOMAN
Super badass

JUSTICE LEAGUE OF AMERICA
DC Comics' super team

BATMAN
Gotham's protector

BATMAN
The Caped Crusader

CATWOMAN
Super feline

SUPERMAN
Cult Kryptonian

I AM . . .
Superman

HULK
Super angry

MARVEL COMICS
Cult comics, cult characters

MARVEL
The biggest family of superheroes

X-MEN
Adored mutants

WOLVERINE
Mutant with steel claws

LUCKY GIRL
Go out with a superhero

THE AVENGERS
Marvel's super team

THE AVENGERS
Distinctive logo

CAPTAIN AMERICA
Leader of the Avengers

IRON MAN
Armored defender

SHELDON AND HIS T-SHIRTS

In *The Big Bang Theory*, the cult geek series, one character in particular does justice to the T-shirt: Sheldon Cooper. With his T-shirts featuring weird and wacky prints, superheroes, and ironic messages, he's a trendsetter without even realizing it.

FUNNY FACES

Pop art has driven the cult of personality to a seriously high level. Warhol may have produced umpteen copies of Marilyn and Jackie, but the pop generation picked up the baton by displaying on their T-shirts the faces of those who made their era. One can even gauge a celebrity's fame thanks to this fashion trend. There can be no true glory without a T-shirt bearing one's effigy. It is much more than fifteen minutes of fame.

KARL LAGERFELD AND CHOUPETTE
Improbable duo

JUSTIN BIEBER
Apologetic singer

ONE DIRECTION
Idolized boy band

ELLE MACPHERSON
Perfect body

KANYE WEST
Outspoken rapper

ANDY WARHOL
Visionary artist

FORD FOR LIFE

KING TOM FORD
Tom Ford is without a doubt one of the designers who appears the most on T-shirts. He has turned his image and his flawless physique into advertising tools, wisely knowing when to throw open the floodgates of publicity and also when to be more discreet. A true pop character.

CHARLIE SHEEN
Hollywood bad boy

WILL SMITH
Hollywood hero

ROBERT PATTINSON
Vampire star

KATE MOSS
Legendary model

LINDSAY LOHAN
Former It Girl

WIZ KHALIFA
Tattooed rapper

PHARRELL WILLIAMS
Hatless singer

MARILYN MONROE
"Pooh pooh bee doo"

JUSTIN BIEBER
Teen heartthrob

MUSTACHIOED CELEBS

The Eleven Paris brand had the genius idea of T-shirts with celebrity faces from the worlds of cinema, music, and fashion, posed with a finger above their lips to reveal a drawn-on mustache. The commercial success was huge, although some of the celebs were less pleased.

LOL!

The T-shirt with a message is a must-have item of the 2010s. You can say almost anything on a T-shirt, from a single cryptic word to an existential phrase. The big winner remains the funny message. Irony, self-deprecation, and student humor—lulz always work better on T-shirts.

FOR YOUR BEST BUDDY

FOR THE FOODIE

FOR THE TEEN

FOR THE MORNING PERSON

FOR THE MUSIC LOVER

FOR THE IRONIC

FOR THE CONNOISSEUR

FOR THE BEER LOVER

FOR THE THIRSTY GUY

FOR THE ENVIRONMENTALIST

FOR THE PARTYGOER

FOR THE HUNGRY FRIEND

FOR THE MISANTHROPE

FOR THE UTOPIST

FOR THE REGRETFUL

FOR THE HONEST

FOR THE BILINGUAL

FOR THE SOCCER MAD

FOR THE GENIUS

FOR THE HIGH SCHOOLER

FOR THE FARMER

FOR THE FASHIONISTA

FOR THE ANIMAL LOVER*

FOR THE VACATIONER

* *Biche* means "doe" in French.

FOR THE AVOIDER OF PROFANITY*

FOR THE IRISH

FOR MARILYN

FOR THE INTERNET OBSESSED

FOR THE LITERAL-MINDED

FOR THE DAREDEVIL

FOR THE FAN

FOR THE AMBITIOUS

FOR THE IRREVERENT

* *Phoque* means "seal" in French.

X-RATED

Sexual provocation and other outrageous messages and images also make for very good T-shirt prints, with pictures often doing the job much better than words. Any proper T-shirt lover surely has at least one in his or her wardrobe, the cause of much hilarity and sometimes shock.

ON THE MILFY WAY

DAMN RIGHT

ENOUGH SAID

LAYMAN

SPOONERISM

EAT ORGANIC

CARTMAN AND HIS BUDDIES
South Park dares to use vulgarity, dark humor, and every kind of provocation, even the smuttiest. So a pair of buttocks is really hardly shocking at all.

COTTON ON SCREEN

Movie theater, television, computer, smartphone, tablet: modern culture cannot avoid the filter of a screen, with ever-present streaming of films, cartoons, and TV series providing a permanent escape to imaginary realities and worlds. It is therefore logical that they have found their way onto T-shirts, and to a massive extent.

MARK OF AN ERA
FILM POSTERS

Movie posters are many things. First and foremost, they are sales and marketing tools, but they are also works of art anchored in our collective memories. Streets and magazines are full of them, and when they eventually become vintage, their creative stock rises even higher.

Jaws, Alien, and *Lolita*—so many different films that we wear on our T-shirts are like little testaments to our time and our own character. Wearing a film T-shirt is essentially an homage, but it also becomes a real sign of recognition. They say you can tell a lot about a person from a simple list of his or her three favorite films. And by displaying one's preferences on a T-shirt, one transmits a little bit of oneself. The *Star Wars* poster will reveal a slight geeky edge, that of *Pulp Fiction* a passion for Quentin Tarantino, and *Gone with the Wind* an unshakable romanticism. Some films have even managed to cross generations. One can wear a *Blues Brothers* T-shirt from age seven to seventy-seven with no shame. One film to define yourself, one T-shirt to affirm it.

JAWS
The cult poster that terrorized an entire generation, making every swim in the sea a traumatic test. It's a legendary image, one that the director Steven Spielberg referenced in *Back to the Future Part II*, which was made by his production company Amblin, when Marty McFly is surprised by a hologram trailer for *Jaws 19* and exclaims, "Shark still looks fake." As fake as it may have looked, it was a phenomenon in the 1970s and 1980s.

BACK TO THE FUTURE
Robert Zemeckis, 1985

FORREST GUMP
Robert Zemeckis, 1994

**THE ROCKY HORROR
PICTURE SHOW**
Jim Sharman, 1975

GONE WITH THE WIND
Victor Fleming, 1939

CASABLANCA
Michael Curtiz, 1942

TITANIC
James Cameron, 1997

PLATOON
Oliver Stone, 1986

ALIEN
Ridley Scott, 1979

THE MASK
Charles Russell, 1994

PULP FICTION
Quentin Tarantino, 1994

JACKIE BROWN
Quentin Tarantino, 1997

INGLOURIOUS BASTERDS
Quentin Tarantino, 2009

ROCKY
John G. Avildsen, 1976

TRAINSPOTTING
Danny Boyle, 1996

JURASSIC PARK
Steven Spielberg, 1993

LOLITA
Stanley Kubrick, 1962

A CLOCKWORK ORANGE
Stanley Kubrick, 1971

FULL METAL JACKET
Stanley Kubrick, 1987

BAD T-SHIRT

In *The Hangover* film trilogy, the character of Alan is a rather clueless guy who gets into all sorts of ridiculous difficulties and has a quite "unique" fashion sense, particularly when it comes to his absurd T-shirts with really cheesy prints.

STAR WARS CRAZY

It's quite a feat to escape the *Star Wars* phenomenon. The world's most famous movie saga of the past forty years shows no signs of slowing down. As in all mass marketing processes, derivative products are legion. And T-shirts, real little trophies for die-hard fans, are part of it.

IN A GALAXY FAR, FAR AWAY . . .

LEIA AND HER ARMY

YODA SAYS

STORMTROOPER POWER

REBEL PRINCESS

THE DARK SIDE

HAN AND CHEWIE, BFFS

VERY DARTH VADER

LOYAL SOLDIER

STORMTROOPER HAKA

STAR WARS, THE POSTER

DARTH ANATOMY

REBEL ALLIANCE

C-3PO + R2-D2 = LOVE

EVIL EMPIRE

R2-D2, ROBOT SWAG

YODA SUPERSTAR

***STAR WARS*, MODERN CLASSIC**

TECHNICOLOR STORMTROOPER

TO BE CONTINUED . . .

THE DARK SIDE OF THE FORCE

HAN SOLO, SEXY HERO

***STAR WARS* BY ADIDAS**

***STAR WARS* BY ADIDAS**

STAR WARS X ADIDAS

The relationship between *Star Wars* and Adidas Originals is a long-running love (and business) affair. Sneakers, sweatshirts, pants, and, above all, T-shirts have been the focus of specific collaborations dedicated to the *Star Wars* franchise. The main characters and the world of the films are depicted with a sporty twist that is all Adidas's own.

FILMS ON T-SHIRTS

A character, an image, or a very recognizable film quote—real film buffs don't need to flaunt the official poster to show their knowledge, and these shirts also make for good conversation starters.

KILL BILL
Quentin Tarantino, 2003/2004

THE HANGOVER PART III
Todd Phillips, 2013

THE BLUES BROTHERS
John Landis, 1980

JAMES BOND
1962-2015

THELMA & LOUISE
Ridley Scott, 1991

THELMA & LOUISE
Ridley Scott, 1991

TOO OLD!
Danny Glover in
Lethal Weapon
(Richard Donner,
1987) plays the old
grouch whom Mel
Gibson is always
dragging into crazy
adventures.
Whenever the going
gets tough, he comes
out with "I'm too old
for this shit!"
In reality the fans
never found
him too old, quite
the opposite.

THE GODFATHER
Francis Ford Coppola, 1972

GREMLINS
Joe Dante, 1984

GHOSTBUSTERS
Ivan Reitman, 1984

FORREST GUMP
Robert Zemeckis, 1994

RESERVOIR DOGS
Quentin Tarantino, 1992

E.T. THE EXTRA-TERRESTRIAL
Steven Spielberg, 1982

THE FIFTH ELEMENT
Luc Besson, 1997

PULP FICTION
Quentin Tarantino, 1994

THE NIGHTMARE BEFORE CHRISTMAS
Henry Selick, 1993

DIRTY DANCING
Emile Ardolino, 1987

BACK TO THE FUTURE PART II
Robert Zemeckis, 1989

GREASE
Randal Kleiser, 1978

DIE HARD
John McTiernan, 1988

BREATHLESS
Jean-Luc Godard, 1960

BREAKFAST AT TIFFANY'S
Blake Edwards, 1961

INDIANA JONES
Steven Spielberg, 1981-2008

MARS ATTACKS!
Tim Burton, 1996

SCREAM
Wes Craven, 1996

CARTOONS!

Cartoon art often makes for fun and colorful T-shirts, whether they are based on famous Disney or Pixar films, or feature more recent characters from TV shows. These fantastic T-shirts are great for both young and old.

LOONEY TUNES
What's up, Doc?

LOONEY TUNES
Tweety and Sylvester

SCOOBY-DOO
Where are you?

CAT'S EYE
Three agile panthers

DRAGON BALL Z
Kamehameha !

SAILOR MOON
Moon Prism Power!

SAILOR MOON
Guardian cats

POKÉMON
Pika pika

SOUTH PARK
Oh my God! They killed Kenny!

THE POWERPUFF GIRLS
Blossom, Bubbles, and Buttercup

SPONGEBOB SQUAREPANTS
And Patrick Star

TOY STORY
To infinity and beyond!

TOY STORY
Little green men

MONSTERS, INC.
Bob Wazowski, elite scarer

DESPICABLE ME
Bananonina!

MICKEY MOUSE CLUB

Disney is all about legendary characters, of which Mickey Mouse and Donald Duck are perhaps the best known. They are a somewhat antithetical duo: Donald, the grumpy duck and Mickey, the feel-good mouse—a fictional pair that serves as a reference point among the narrative frameworks of cartoons and favorite toys for children of all eras.

MICKEY MOUSE
The original

MICKEY MOUSE
Rock, paper, scissors

ALICE IN WONDERLAND
Revisited by Marc Jacobs

*SNOW WHITE AND
THE SEVEN DWARFS*
Someday my prince will come

BAMBI
The most famous fawn

THE LION KING
Hakuna matata

THE LITTLE MERMAID
Under the sea with Ariel

FROZEN
Let it go!

THE PRINCESSES
Acting goofy

TV SHOWS

Television shows have been a major element of screen culture, and crystallized the narrative possibilities of the modern era. It is, therefore, quite proper that each one should be immortalized on a T-shirt that inspires nostalgia for a particular era.

BEWITCHED
Sarcastic Endora

STAR TREK
Vulcan salute

CHARLIE'S ANGELS
Dynamic trio

MAGNUM, P.I.
Thomas Magnum and his mustache

BAYWATCH
Pamela Anderson, aka C.J. Parker

FAMILY MATTERS
Steve Urkel

**DYLAN, 1990s
HEARTTHROB**
*Beverly Hills,
90210*, the hit teen
show of the 1990s!
While Brandon
Walsh was the
clean-cut guy next
door, Dylan McKay
was a bit of a bad
boy, mysterious
and sexy, which
obviously made
Brenda and Kelly
crazy about him,
along with
thousands of
infatuated teenage
girls, even if they
lived on the other
side of the world
from Beverly Hills.

RED WEDDING
On episode nine
of season three of
Game of Thrones,
a host of characters
were massacred
at a wedding and
shocked fans, some
of whom still
haven't gotten over
it. So what better
way to exorcise the
trauma than
through humor.
This most bloody
of weddings is
immortalized on
an ironic T-shirt,
itself a riff on an
old T-shirt slogan.

THE SIMPSONS
Homer's beer

THE FRESH PRINCE OF BEL-AIR
Will (Smith)

THE NANNY
Grandma Yetta

FRIENDS
The whole gang

BUFFY THE VAMPIRE SLAYER
Buffy Summers

MALCOLM IN THE MIDDLE
The family

HOW I MET YOUR MOTHER
Barney Stinson

DEXTER
Dexter Morgan

BREAKING BAD
Walter White

GAME OF THRONES,
BEYOND THE WALL

It is *THE* cult series of the past few years, complete with its own range of merchandising, including T-shirts featuring characters, famous lines of dialogue, and coats of arms of the key families. Fans rush to buy them, as they wait eagerly for the next episode, forgetting (a little) that "the night is dark and full of terrors."

HOUSE STARK ANNOUNCES WINTER

HOUSE LANNISTER ROARS

HOUSE TARGARYEN, DRAGON TAMERS

HOUSE BARATHEON, KINGS OF FURY

HOUSE GREYJOY, HOUSE OF YARA AND THEON

HOUSE TULLY MOURNS

**HOUSE TYRELL,
GUARDIANS OF HIGHGARDEN**

**HOUSE ARRYN,
IN THEIR IMPREGNABLE EYRIE**

**HOUSE MORMONT,
LOYAL TO HOUSE STARK**

**HOUSE CLEGANE,
LOYAL TO HOUSE LANNISTER**

WHITE WALKERS, THE "OTHERS"

**AND THINGS WILL GO
TERRIBLY WRONG**

THE CROWS ATTACK

LADY MORMONT, TOO

HODOR!

TO SERVE YOU

. . . BUT YOU SHALL BECOME KING

SENSE OF PRIORITIES

EACH MAN HAS AN EXPERTISE

HAND OF THE KING

THE OPPOSITE OF JON SNOW

. . . AND PAY THEIR DEBTS

IT'S NOT THE SAME!

A PREDICTABLE ENDING?

KHALEESI, BETTER THAN OBAMA?

DRINK OF CHAMPIONS

A LARGE FAMILY

THE FAB FOUR OF WESTEROS

THUG LIFE

REGICIDE

LADY-KILLER

GOOD NEWS

ALCOHOL OF THE NORTH

TRIBE

IDENTITY T-SHIRTS

Tell me what you're wearing and I'll tell you who you are. The adage applies perfectly to the T-shirt, which, over time, has become the banner of all our assertions. Beyond political statements, the T-shirt and what's printed on it is a true reflection of our personality, even our identity, our belonging. Regionalism, nationalism, individualism, professional tribe, identity affirmation—they can all be displayed on a T-shirt.

I AM . . .

. . . ANYTHING AND EVERYTHING

I am what I wear. And I say that because I am proud of the fact, whether it's a joke, whether it makes me stand out, or whether it's for self-affirmation, perhaps without me even knowing it. Whatever the reason, and even when it seems entirely cryptic, I am never really somebody else on a T-shirt.

Perhaps it's a result of the recession, but modern society is composed in such a way that the individual has a strong tendency to withdraw into themselves. They deal with the problems of the contemporary world—a civilization lacking points of reference and a modernity that tends to erase humanity—by reaffirming their personality, their individuality, in short, their deeper self. Whether through humor or the enunciation of more serious realities, the need to say "I am" or "I am not" is symptomatic of a desire to stand out at all costs. "I am complicated," "I am a unicorn," and "I am not a morning person"—all these seemingly insignificant phrases reveal an ego that's perhaps a bit mistreated by the twenty-first century, an ego seeking to emancipate itself. The message is often short, since it must be read quickly and hit the nail on the head. It may initially seem superficial, yet it always says something more important. What could be more practical and more prominent than displaying this expression of identity on one's T-shirt? The T-shirt thus becomes our initial means of communication upon meeting a person for the first time. For in the end, when you say, "I am X" to others, you are also asking them who they are.

I AM OTHER
I Am Other is a creative collective that serves as an umbrella for Pharrell Williams' various endeavors. Fashion, music, and video—the more varied the media, the happier the producer. The concept is a different vision of the cultural landscape, one that attracted the Japanese brand Uniqlo, with whom Williams has collaborated, notably on T-shirts.

STAR SYSTEM

A T-shirt with your own face on it—that's
the apotheosis of star attitude. Miley
Cyrus and Paris Hilton didn't get it
wrong, the former with street bling,
the latter with more of a provocative style.
Now that's an ego trip.

I LIKE TO BE CLEAR

I CONFESS

I ROCK

I LOVE FRANCE

I MASTER THE FLOW

I REFUSE THE TRUTH

I AM IN A RELATIONSHIP

I COME FROM JAPAN

I AM LYING

I DON'T LIKE TO GO OUT

I AM BILINGUAL

I AM NO PERFECTIONIST

I HAVE HIDDEN DEPTHS

I AM NOT PUNCTUAL

I AM A MICHAEL JACKSON FAN

I CONTRADICT MYSELF *

I AM IN CONTROL

I GET UP LATE

* "It's simple, I'm complicated."

BACK TO SCHOOL

To wear the T-shirt of one's university is to reveal something of one's own history and personality. A real American tradition, the college T-shirt is a way of remaining connected to one's student past. People keep them for many years after they graduate, and it even becomes a kind of trophy.

HARVARD UNIVERSITY, MASSACHUSETTS
The oldest

MIT, MASSACHUSETTS
Geeky

PRINCETON UNIVERSITY, NEW JERSEY
Preppy

UC BERKELEY, CALIFORNIA
Hippy

BERKLEE COLLEGE OF MUSIC, MASSACHUSETTS
Musical

BROWN UNIVERSITY, RHODE ISLAND
Environmental leadership

YALE UNIVERSITY, CONNECTICUT
Hillary Clinton's alma mater

WHARTON SCHOOL, PENNSYLVANIA
Business brains

**STANFORD UNIVERSITY,
CALIFORNIA**
Silicon Valley

COLUMBIA UNIVERSITY, NEW YORK
New York institution

UCLA, CALIFORNIA
Hollywood

**DUKE UNIVERSITY,
NORTH CAROLINA**
Basketball friendly

**UNIVERSITY OF NOTRE DAME,
INDIANA**
Football fans

OBERLIN COLLEGE, OHIO
Edgy underground

**SARAH LAWRENCE COLLEGE,
NEW YORK**
Arty

FLAG BEARERS

The flag—supreme symbol of belonging. Whether it is national, regional, or simply local, it can be a sign of pride and self-affirmation. The flag indicates one's original or adopted land, and is part of an individual's identity. To display it is to reveal a bit of oneself.

STARS AND STRIPES
United States

TRICOLOR
Mexico

UNION JACK
United Kingdom

RED DRAGON
Wales

KANGAROO LAND
Australia

SUNNY BANNER
Jamaica

HEXAGON
France

MOOR'S HEAD
Corsica

IKURRIÑA
Basque Country

GWENN-HA-DU
Brittany

GERMAN FEDERAL STATE OF . . .
. . .Bavaria

IBERIAN REPUBLIC
Portugal

NORTH AFRICAN KINGDOM
Morocco

SYMBOLIC FLAG
Republic of South Africa

FIVE-STAR RED FLAG
People's Republic of China

FORCES OF THE UNITED STATES

FBI, CIA, and NYPD—we all know these abbreviations and the professions they represent. Wearing one's organization on a T-shirt is another way, in addition to the uniform, of registering one's belonging to a group and showing one's pride in it, particularly when it's a job that comes with some risk attached. You don't need to be a member to show your support.

**NEW YORK CITY
POLICE DEPARTMENT**

**FIRE DEPARTMENT OF
THE CITY OF NEW YORK**

LIFEGUARD

**FEDERAL BUREAU OF
INVESTIGATION**

CENTRAL INTELLIGENCE AGENCY

NATIONAL SECURITY AGENCY

US ARMY

VIETNAM VETERANS

US AIR FORCE

THE NATIONAL GUARD

US COAST GUARD

US MARINE CORPS

US NAVY

NAVY SEALS

SPECIAL WEAPONS AND TACTICS

TEAM UNIFORMS

The T-shirt is inseparable from sports. A stage costume for nearly all athletes, the T-shirt or sports shirt is both a practical and a symbolic garment. The focus of much technical development in terms of comfort and ergonomics, it is, above all, worn to honor one's team or country. Wear it with pride.

SOCCER SHIRT

MYTHOLOGY OF A T-SHIRT

The soccer shirt is undoubtedly the best-known sports T-shirt in the world, and it is due to the fact that soccer is the most played sport on the planet. Take a close look at social media or improvised soccer games and you'll always see a soccer shirt worn like a second skin. Here's a look at the craziest shirts.

Soaked with sweat, sometimes blood, the soccer shirt is a totemic object for soccer players. They pull it over their head to celebrate a goal, hurl it into the stands to reward an ardent fan, kiss their club's logo placed over the heart, strike it with their fist as if possessed, and even exchange it with a player from the opposing side at the end of the game. The soccer shirt possesses strength, courage, and genius that transform players into real modern Samsons. And they themselves believe it! You only have to watch the persistence with which Zlatan Ibrahimović fought to win the number 10 shirt at Paris Saint-Germain, a number worn by so many prestigious players in so many top teams before him. Yes, soccer shirts are real trophies. With stars to indicate victory and names of the most illustrious players marked out with flock printing, soccer fans rush to stores to claim a piece of their favorite players by purchasing a shirt. From a business point of view, the soccer shirt is a gold mine, something that the uniform manufacturers have long understood. Some shirts become really popular, commanding high prices. After the 1998 World Cup, there was a huge appetite for soccer shirts with a woman's cut, and the companies making them were swift to take advantage of these new recruits and this new income stream.

SOCCER FASHION
In 2011, Nike, the manufacturer for the France team's uniform, chose a striped shirt for away games. And eleven guys looking just a bit like sailors caused quite a buzz. The innovation wasn't to everybody's taste, but it did get everyone talking.

MEXICO, 1998
The shirt of the
Mexico national
team honors the
founding legend
of the Aztecs.
These ancestors
remain very dear
to Mexicans today.

COLORADO CARIBOUS
(United States) 1978

AJAX AMSTERDAM
(Netherlands) 1990 – away

MANCHESTER UNITED
(England) 1991 – away

READING
(England) 1992 – away

ATALANTA
(Italy) 1994 – away

MADUREIRA
(Brazil) 1994

SHAMROCK ROVERS
(Ireland) 1994 – away

NOTTS COUNTY
(England) 1995 – away

SCUNTHORPE UNITED
(England) 1995 – away

HULL CITY
(England) 1994

BARCELONA
(Spain) 1997 – away

BOCHUM
(Germany) 1998

JAGUARES DE CHIAPAS
(Mexico) 2003

ATHLETIC BILBAO
(Spain) 2004

OLYMPIQUE LYONNAIS
(France) 2011 – away

CHARLEROI
(Belgium) 2013

RECREATIVO DE HUELVA
(Spain) 2013 – away

BRISTOL ROVERS
(England) 1994 – away

DERBY COUNTY
(England) 1994 – away

EINTRACHT FRANKFURT
(Germany) 1994

**OLYMPIQUE
DE MARSEILLE**
(France) 2008 – away

CHELSEA
(England) 1995 – away

JAMAICA
(national team) 1997

MEXICO
(national team) 1999
– goalkeeper

CROATIA
(national team) 1996
– goalkeeper

BEYOND SOCCER

There is more to life than soccer. Every sport, from tennis to rugby to basketball, has its shirt, and everyone sees in it a way to affirm their identity. Players wear very distinctive shirts, whether for aesthetic reasons, as the French tennis player Jo-Wilfried Tsonga did in 2016, or for the purposes of a particular event, such as the legendary yellow jersey of the Tour de France cycling race.

TENNIS
Andy Murray, 2009

TENNIS
Richard Gasquet, 2014

TENNIS
Novak Djokovic, 2016

TENNIS
Rafael Nadal, 2014

TENNIS
Roger Federer, 2015

TENNIS
Jo-Wilfried Tsonga, 2016

RUGBY
All Blacks, New Zealand, 2016

RUGBY
France national team, 2016

RUGBY
England national team, 2016

TOUR DE FRANCE
Race leader, 2016

TOUR DE FRANCE
Leader in the points classification, 2016

TOUR DE FRANCE
King of the Mountains, 2016

HANDBALL
France, 2016

HANDBALL
Paris Saint-Germain, 2016

HANDBALL
Club Atlético Madrid, 2016

SUPPORTERS' T-SHIRTS

The relationship between fashion and sports is not limited to professional sportswear; it extends to casual, cotton T-shirts. More practical to wear than a sports jersey, and suitable for everyday wear, these T-shirts are objects that all fans can buy themselves, whether they support a team, a player, or even just a particular event.

PARIS SAINT-GERMAIN
France – soccer

OLYMPIQUE DE MARSEILLE
France – soccer

AS SAINT-ÉTIENNE
France – soccer

REAL MADRID
Spain – soccer

CHELSEA
England – soccer

MANCHESTER UNITED
England – soccer

WORLD CHAMPIONS

In 1998, France hosted the FIFA World Cup. There was an official logo, official song, official mascot, many other goodies, and, of course, an official T-shirt. In a miracle final, France beat Brazil 3–0, and any item dating from that period now has the status of a holy relic in France.

TOKYO OLYMPICS

In 1964, Asia hosted the legendary sporting institution that is the Olympic Games for the very first time. And it happened in Tokyo. On this T-shirt, the red circle that appears on the Japanese flag is placed above the Olympic rings. It is now a collector's item.

CHICAGO BULLS
United States – basketball

LOS ANGELES LAKERS
United States – basketball

SAN ANTONIO SPURS
United States – basketball

LIONEL MESSI
Argentina – soccer

ZLATAN IBRAHIMOVIĆ
Sweden – soccer

TONY PARKER
France – basketball

ROGER FEDERER
Switzerland – tennis

BJÖRN BORG
Sweden – tennis

USAIN BOLT
Jamaica – track and field

SPORTS BRANDS

Sports brands use T-shirts not just for sporting purposes, but also as promotional tools. T-shirts serve as uniforms for top players and also as street fashion pieces. Big logos and trendy designs are obviously all part and parcel.

CHAMPION
Winning since 1919

UMBRO
Made in England since 1924

FILA
Founded in Italy in 1911

LACOSTE
Legendary crocodile since 1933

ASICS
Made in Japan since 1949

EVERLAST
All for the noble art since 1910

NIKE
The Swoosh, legendary logo since 1971

NIKE
Omnipresent since 1964

NIKE
Punchy slogan since 1988

NIKE
Motivated since 1964

NIKE
Modest pride since 1964

ADIDAS
Original since 1949

ADIDAS
Streetwear since 1949

ADIDAS
Eye-catching logo since 1949

ADIDAS
Sexy sport since 1949

LEGENDARY HAIRSTYLES
To celebrate the 2014 World Cup, which was held in Brazil, Le coq sportif decided to pay homage to the rather kitsch hairstyles of several soccer players. Here we see the wavy hair of Johan Cruyff and Sócrates's famous headband.

FASHION VICTIM

ON THE
RED CARPET

If the T-shirt was originally just a utilitarian undergarment, it soon became a highly identifiable fashion item. T-shirts are now made by everyone in the fashion world, from luxury empires to small-scale designers, by way of fast fashion and arty labels. The fashionistas are crazy for them, sales are still good, and the creative possibilities are endless. A simple logo is sometimes enough to make one an "It" piece, the star of social media and the red carpets. In short, the T-shirt has never been so trendy.

KING OF THE CATWALKS

THE POP MOSCHINO T-SHIRT

The sensation of the 2015 Milan Fashion Week was, without a doubt, the Moschino show. Things have been crazy ever since cool kid Jeremy Scott took over as art director at the Italian brand.

Jeremy Scott's genius idea was to produce items with very strong visual and brand identity that would be highly "shoppable" and ready to wear. The big winner of this collection was the T-shirt. And not just any T-shirt, but a series emblematic of the season, each one reproducing an element of pop culture: Barbie, McDonald's, Super Mario, and also teddy bears and window cleaning products—anything that was part of daily life had become wonderfully trendy. And it was all done with a touch of luxurious irony. Available on the brand's online store at the end of the show, the T-shirts (and the smartphone cases) became promotional emblems of sorts for the collection. Cheaper than the more "serious" pieces, easy to mix and match with one's own clothes, and a true "likes" magnet on social media, the Moschino T-shirts have become cult pieces, just like a Chanel bag or a pair of Adidas Stan Smiths. The collection has won many converts, from young bloggers to experienced fashion editors, and their Instagram accounts are full of snaps worthy of a Warhol silkscreen print. Visually, it's funny; intellectually, it's almost art; and commercially, it's very clever. In short, it's pop.

POP DESIGNER
Since 2013, the art director of the iconic Italian fashion house Moschino has been the talented bad boy Jeremy Scott. He is the driving force behind a new, younger, crazier, and more pop direction—a fun approach to fashion that is evident on the brand's T-shirts.

UNIVERSAL LANGUAGE

MOSCHINO BARBIE, BLONDE

MOSCHINO BARBIE, BRUNETTE

SUPER MARIO FASHIONISTA

STYLIZED SPONGEBOB SQUAREPANTS

TOY MADE IN ITALY

COUTURE ON A HANGER

IT'S IN THE BOX

100% MOSCHINO

READY TO BEAR

**CAN FASHION SERIOUSLY
DAMAGE YOUR HEALTH?**

STREET ART

CATWALK CAR WASH

FRESH, EAU DE TOILETTE

COLORBLOCK PRINT

THIS IS NOT A TOY!

CARTOON CHIC

POP JEWELS

HIGH LUXURY

It cannot be denied that luxury brands love T-shirts. In spite of their very high-end image, they always return to the timeless T-shirt, redesigning it in genius ways. Whether just a simple logo, a means of reaffirming an identity, or a more sophisticated design, one thing is for sure: the prices of these luxury T-shirts can sometimes leave one speechless.

ALEXANDER MCQUEEN

BURBERRY GUARDSMAN

MARC JACOBS SHOPPING BAG

DOLCE & GABBANA MAMA

CHRISTIAN DIOR SLOGAN

FENDI EYES

SAINT LAURENT VACATION PRINT

MARY KATRANTZOU JEWELRY PRINT

VERSACE BAROQUE PRINT

STELLA MCCARTNEY PANTHERS

KENZO TIGER

GIVENCHY GORILLAS

YVES SAINT LAURENT LOGO

LANVIN BYE-BYE

BALMAIN LOGO WITH H&M

ALWAYS IN VOGUE

Some patterns appear on T-shirts in all collections: polka dots big or small, in black and white or in color; Scottish tartans; graphic prints; Liberty prints; hypnotic checks; big, exotic flowers; hippie tie-dye; and even wallpaper. These are the prints that have remained favorites over the years.

CAMOUFLAGE
by Valentino

CAMOUFLAGE
by Neil Barrett

CAMOUFLAGE
by Valentino

TIE-DYE
by Wasted

TIE-DYE
by DSquared2

TIE-DYE
by Hype

DIRECTION
HAWAII
Tropical flowers were a very popular motif of the 1980s, largely thanks to Tom Selleck in the unforgettable TV series *Magnum, P.I.* Today they are making a big comeback in the fashion world, and it is not uncommon to see them on the coolest T-shirts.

LIBERTY SPIRIT
Originally, Liberty
was a fabric
developed by
Arthur Liberty in
the late nineteenth
century. It is so thin
that one can see the
print on the reverse
side as well as the
front. By extension,
"Liberty print" now
refers to any very
dense floral print.
Bucolic and chic.

STRIPES
by Petit Bateau

STRIPES
by 1789 Cala

STRIPES
by Isabel Marant Étoile

POLKA DOTS
by Le Mont Saint Michel

POLKA DOTS
by WE

POLKA DOTS
by Red Valentino

CHECKS
by Rag & Bone

CHECKS
by Victoria Beckham

CHECKS
by Lanvin

SMALL DESIGNERS, BIG T-SHIRTS

The T-shirt is the canvas of choice for small designers. New fashion talents love this garment since it offers them a way to showcase their most inventive designs. Animals, fruits, drawings, stylized logos, humorous messages, and customizable embroideries—designer T-shirts are as cool as they are varied.

MARKUS LUPFER LOGO

ISABEL MARANT LOGO

MARC JACOBS EMOJI

ZOE KARSSEN MESSAGE

AU JOUR LE JOUR IRON

PETER JENSEN DESSERT

TSUMORI CHISATO SUPERGIRL

DSQUARED2 PORTRAIT

CARVEN POSTCARD

ALEXANDER WANG BARCODE

A.P.C. PROMISE

ED HARDY SKULL

NO/ONE PARIS PLAY ON WORDS*

MSGM POP HEART

MONCLER X AMI LOGO

* Belleville is a neighborhood in Paris.

N° 21 ANCHOR

THE ACADEMY NEW YORK IDOL

SANDRO APPLAUSE

PHILIPP PLEIN GRAPHIC PRINT

ETRO PARROT

ÊTRE CÉCILE SKI TRIP

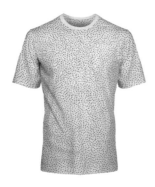

**COMMUNE DE PARIS 1871
POINTILLIST**

TH GALLERY ZEN

CARVEN CASSETTE

FAITH CONNEXION COAT OF ARMS

CIVISSUM ID

1789 CALA CLUB

SLEEPY JONES BLAZER

FILLES À PAPA GANG

ZOE KARSSEN COURTESY

VETEMENTS HELLO

A.P.C. PHOTO

BALZAC PARIS COUPLE

AGNÈS B.

Since 1975, Agnès Troublé, known as "agnès b.," has been designing clothes that are minimalist, chic, and timeless, including best sellers such as the snap cardigan. She has also designed a number of T-shirts, featuring some of her favorite motifs, including the heart, the salamander, and the irony mark. Her T-shirts also serve as blank canvases for the artists she continues to support.

SIGNATURE

SALAMANDER

COLLABORATION WITH BENOIT JAMMES

COLLABORATION WITH ELLI MEDEIROS

COLLABORATION WITH BENOIT JAMMES

COLLABORATION WITH JEAN-MICHEL BASQUIAT

POSTCARD

STRIPES XS

STRIPES XL

YOU GOT IT OR YOU DON'T!*

ROCK ON

CINEMA FOR LIFE

**COLLABORATION
WITH SÉBASTIEN PRESCHOUX**

**GRAPHIC AND GEOMETRIC,
THE WAVE**

**GRAPHIC AND GEOMETRIC,
THE TRIANGLE**

* *Niaque* is a French slang meaning tenacity/determination/motivation.

IRONY MARK

STAR

**COLLABORATION WITH
RAFAEL GRAY**

**COLLABORATION WITH
GUS VAN SANT**

**COLLABORATION WITH
SEYDOU KEÏTA**

ROSES

COLLABORATION WITH JAY ONE

**COLLABORATION WITH
JULIEN NÉDÉLEC**

A HEART FOR SARAJEVO

COLLABORATION WITH MP5

COLLABORATION WITH TONY IACOPONELLI

COLLABORATION WITH JULIEN LANGENDORFF

COLLABORATION WITH ELZO

"WE WANT IMAGINATION IN POWER!!"

COLLABORATION WITH PIERRE BORDIN

COLLABORATION WITH BENOIT JAMMES

COLLABORATION WITH JULIEN LANGENDORFF

COLLABORATION WITH CLAUDE LÉVÊQUE

WEAR CREATIVITY

T-shirts can display many different types of artwork, from painting to sculpture to prints, be they by old masters, contemporary artists, or up-and-coming talents. Sometimes a particular T-shirt will attain iconic status as an artwork in its own right, proving once again the creative potential of a simple cotton T-shirt.

ARTWORKS ON T-SHIRTS

T-SHIRTS AT THE MUSEUM

The T-shirt as an artwork. Or perhaps merely the canvas for it? From incredibly famous works to lesser known ones, T-shirts have become museum pieces in their own right.

The T-shirt is a cultural object, bearer of numerous images and messages related to the cultural sector, whatever they may be. But looking deeper, there exists a real link between T-shirts and the art world, one that almost gives the humble T-shirt a more noble aspect. In museum shops, it has become quite common to see T-shirts sold alongside exhibition catalogs, coffee-table books, cards, and bookmarks. They are souvenirs we bring back from an exhibition we've just seen. They bear the mark of an artist, or depict a painting, a sculpture, or an installation. Wearing these T-shirts is a contribution to artistic expression. When an artwork is only partially shown, and it is more of an allusion, the T-shirt becomes part of an artistic game, placing the wearer in a more complex cultural reality, for whoever can identify the clue. T-shirts are also ways for young artists to express themselves and to get their work much better known. Some of these T-shirts become almost as treasured as the original artworks they depict, a means for the ordinary person to own something that would normally be out of reach.

ARTY SHIRTS
The works of Jean-Michel Basquiat have had a kind of second life on T-shirts these last few years. As the artist's popularity continues to rise, the fashion industry has made the most of this success, turning Basquiat's graffiti and paintings into prints. Here, in the window of a Gap store, we can see how Basquiat's uncompromising art has become mainstream.

JEAN-MICHEL BASQUIAT
Graffiti

JEAN-MICHEL BASQUIAT
Dinosaur

JEAN-MICHEL BASQUIAT
Street music

HOKUSAI
The Great Wave off Kanagawa

BOTTICELLI
The Birth of Venus

HENRI MATISSE
Dance

ANDY WARHOL
Campbell's Soup Cans

ANDY WARHOL
Campbell's Soup Cans, Cow, and *Flowers*

ÉDOUARD MANET
Portrait of Méry Laurent

SARAH MORRIS
Globo

YAYOI KUSAMA
Collection exhibited at MoMA

PAULA SCHER
Poster for the Public Theater in New York

JACKSON POLLOCK
Blind Spots

JEFF KOONS
Balloon Rabbit

RENÉ MAGRITTE
The Treachery of Images

VASSILY KANDINSKY
Improvisation. Gorge

PABLO PICASSO
The Weeping Woman

PAUL GAUGUIN
Delightful Land

KEITH HARING, FROM STREET TO T-SHIRT

Simple shapes in bright colors edged in black display an optimism and a joyful creative force. Keith Haring's creations have their roots in the street, long before he became a favorite with art dealers. Covering the subway, sidewalks, and walls, Haring's street art takes its inspiration from New Yorkers' everyday lives. It's only natural that his artworks would make their way onto the classic everyday garment.

HEART

RADIANT BABY

BABY ON SHOULDERS

NY APPLE

NEW YORK CITY

STATUE OF LIBERTY

Keith Haring shows his support for the Great Peace March of 1986, a movement calling for nuclear disarmament, whose participants walked from Los Angeles to Washington, D.C.

The "art of the real" of the 1950s and 1960s was a concept dear to Keith Haring, who drove his art to merge with the street. Subway walls and sidewalk slabs became covered with the artist's works. In the early 1980s, New York galleries went mad for Haring, turning him into a true star of contemporary art.

THE BARKING DOG

UPSIDE-DOWN FIGURES

SPLIT

SELF-PORTRAIT

DANCING FIGURE

THE DOG AND HIS TAIL

FLAG

ANGEL RIDING A DOG

SMILING HEART

ART: RIFFS AND PARODIES ON T-SHIRTS

Art also finds its way onto T-shirts through riff and parody: messages, humorous designs, artist portraits, or references for the cognoscenti. These T-shirts are nods to the art world, and end up becoming artworks in their own right. Very clever, very cool.

DIRTY JOB

THAT IS THE QUESTION

"THE ART OF NOTHING"

DALÍ, GAZE AND MUSTACHE

PICASSO IN A KAFFIYEH

FRIDA, ELECTRO GIRL

YEEZY + GAUGUIN

DRESSED LIKE VENUS

DANCERS PRACTICING AT THE BARRE, FERGALICIOUS VERSION

REBEL ARTHUR

BAUDELAIRE SAYS . . .

RIHANNA SAYS . . .

FRANCIS AND WILLIAM

FOREVER MARCEL

POP GANG

ALFRED DE MUSSET SAYS . . .*

EMBROIDERED BAUDELAIRE**

PROUST'S MADELEINE***

HAMLET'S QUESTION 2.0

SEXY DAVID

ANATOMICAL *VENUS DE MILO*

HIPSTER MONA LISA

MONA LEIA

MOZART, HEART OF A ROCKER

* "Never mind the bottle, as long as it gets you drunk." / ** *The Flowers of Evil*, a famous collection of poetry by Charles Baudelaire. /
*** A reference to Marcel Proust's series of autobiographical novels, where the taste of a madeleine cake triggers a flood of memories.

EIGHTEENTH-CENTURY SLAM

GUERNICA **IN CHICAGO**

AMY LICHTENSTEIN

INSPIRATION LICHTENSTEIN

POP TRAGEDY

POP QUESTION

WATCH THE BALLOON DOG RUN

PARTY'S OVER

HISTORY OF ART IN NINE STAGES

PORTRAIT OF THE AUTHOR

IN T-SHIRTS

We all know that a T-shirt is more than just a piece of cotton.
It is a facet of our personality. So here is a portrait of the author,
Raphaëlle Orsini, in T-shirts.

MY CITY
Paris

MY ORIGIN
Corsica

MY CURRENT SLOGAN
Hill Yes!

MY FAVORITE CHOREOGRAPHY
Single Ladies, Beyoncé

MY SPORTS NOSTALGIA
France, FIFA World Cup champions 1998

MY TEEN SERIES
Beverly Hills, 90210

NOBODY PUTS BABY IN THE CORNER

MY FAVORITE MOVIE LINE
Dirty Dancing

MY JOKEY FASHION

Is style just a point of view?

CONTENTS

ACKNOWLEDGMENTS

Copyright Éditions would like to thank all of the brands depicted in this book, including Adidas, agnès b., Amazon, American Apparel, Blueinc, Eleven Paris, Être Cécile, Farfetch, Fed-corp, Kickz, Mapmystate, Monsieur T-shirt, MyTheresa, Net-à-porter, Nike, Nycwebstore, Rad, Red Bubble, Serishirts, Smallable, Sotshirt, Spreadshirt, SPRZNY, Theshirtlist, Tshirtgameofthrones, Uniqlo, Urbanshirts, Weheartgeeks, and Zazzle.

The author would like to thank Gabrielle Lafarge and Laurène Saby; Sara Quémener, Mathilde Boisserie, and Claudie Souchet for their patience and good ideas; Clément Crépu for his soccer insights; Dad, Mom, and Maxime; and Thomas Figueiredo.

IMAGE CREDITS

All visuals: © DR, except: p. 1: © Terry O'Neill/Hulton Archive/Getty Images; pp. 2–3: © Spencer Platt/Getty Images/AFP; p. 4: © Christian Vierig/Getty Images; p. 5: © Karl Prouse/Catwalking/Getty Images; p. 6: © Matt Cardy/Getty Images/AFP; p. 7: © 40 Acres & A Mule/20th Century Fox/The Kobal Collection/Aurimages; p. 19: © John Engstead/ John Kobal Foundation/Getty Images; p. 20: © Eliot Elisofon/The LIFE Picture Collection/Getty Images; p. 21: © Bettmann/Getty Images; p. 27: © DR American Apparel; p. 33: © Heilemann/Gamma-Rapho; p. 40: © Archive Photos/Getty Images; p. 41: © Christopher Simon Sykes/Hulton Archive/Getty Images; p. 45: © Dennis Morris/ Camera Press/Gamma-Rapho; p. 62: © Ke.Mazur/WireImage/Getty Images; p. 63: © Paul Natkin/WireImage/Getty Images; p. 73: © Paul Morigi/WireImage via Getty Images; p. 79: Ullstein Bild/Getty Images; p. 88: © Noel Vasquez/GC Images/Getty Images; p. 89: Camera Press/Gallo Images/Foto24/Gamma-Rapho; p. 100: © Tim Clayton/Corbis via Getty Images; pp. 146, 147, 164–165: © Rue des Archives/Everett; p. 190: © Kevin Mazur/ WireImage; p. 191: Jean Baptiste Lacroix/WireImage; p. 203: © Dave Winter/Icon Sport; p. 219: © Venturelli/WireImage via Getty Images; p. 239: © Robert Alexander/Getty Images; p. 243: © Ron Galella, Ltd. WireImage via Getty Images; p. 244: © Louis Liotta/ New York Post Archives/© NYP Holdings, Inc. via Getty Images.

Captions for Pages 1 to 7
Page 1 : Spike Lee and his "Peace, Ya Dig" T-shirt. **Pages 2-3 :** T-shirt displaying the names of the forty-nine people killed at Pulse nightclub in Orlando on June 12, 2016. **Page 4 :** Fashion Week goes street style, with the most popular model being the DHL one. **Page 5 :** Jean Paul Gaultier's legendary sailor's T-shirt, which suits both girls and boys. **Page 6 :** The Brexit referendum divided the United Kingdom in June 2016, but those who voted to leave the European Union won the day. **Page 7 :** A particularly ironic Naomi Campbell in Spike Lee's *Girl 6* (1996).